THOMAS MOORE

Dark Eros

The Imagination of Sadism

Second Revised Edition
featuring
an Afterword by the Author
and
a Foreword by Adolf Guggenbühl-Craig

Spring Publications
Woodstock, Connecticut

Published by Spring Publications, Inc.;
299 East Quassett Road;
Woodstock, Connecticut 06281.
Text printed on acid-free paper in Canada.
Third printing of the Second Revised Edition 1999.
Cover design and artwork of this revised edition
by Margot McLean and Slobodan Trajkovic.

Library of Congress Cataloging-in-Publication Data

Moore, Thomas, 1940-
Dark eros : the imagination of Sadism/Thomas Moore.
p. cm.
Includes bibliographical references.
ISBN 0-88214-365-4
1. Sade, marquis de, 1740-1814—Fictional works. 2. Erotic stories, French-History and criticism. 3. Sadism in literature. I. Title.

PQ2063.S3M6 1994
843'.6—dc20 94-35587
CIP

The Mock Turtle, the Gryphon, and Alice were discussing education:

"I only took the regular course."

"What was that?" inquired Alice.

"Reeling and Writhing, of course, to begin with," the Mock Turtle replied: "and then the different branches of Arithmetic—Ambition, Distraction, Uglification and Derision."

"I never heard of 'Uglification,'" Alice ventured to say. "What is it?"

The Gryphon lifted up both its paws in surprise. "Never heard of uglifying!" it exclaimed. "You know what to beautify is, I suppose?"

"Yes," said Alice doubtfully: "it means—to—make—anything—prettier."

"Well then," the Gryphon went on, "if you don't know what to uglify is, you *are* a simpleton."

Alice's Adventures in Wonderland

Contents

Foreword

Many people have heard of the Marquis de Sade and his writings, but very few have ever read his books. Not only because they are not so easy to get—in libraries they are often in closed cupboards—but also because if somebody eventually starts reading de Sade he or she usually stops pretty soon. As Thomas Moore mentions, the Marquis de Sade's writing can appear very boring and monotonous.

Among some sophisticated intellectuals, de Sade has become a cult figure. But these enthusiasts can rarely explain what is supposed to be so great about this French writer. Is he not just a perverted pornographer? What is so special about his works? What can be stimulating about the endless description of every imaginable possibility of sexual and moral perversion? The average psychologist and some clergymen strongly stand for sexuality as an expression of human relationship. De Sade, however, insists on a completely impersonal sexuality. The libertines, both men and women, in de Sade's writings are delighted by anything which repulses the average person. He goes so far as to advocate eating one's excrements to become a feces gourmand. Innocent, beautiful girls have to be tortured, degraded, and corrupted, children disposed of, family ties ignored: any kind of personal eros is strictly taboo among the Sadeian fraternities and sororities.

No one else I know succeeds as does Thomas Moore in showing so convincingly that nobody interested in psychology or even in culture in general should ignore the Marquis de Sade. Moore even goes so far as to show that every human being should be in touch with his own Sadeian side.

Most cultures and religions stress—rightly—morality and decency. "*Hilfreich sei der Mensch, edel und gut*" (Human beings should be helpful, noble, and good), says Goethe. The movement of enlightenment has as its aim the decent, good, altruistic, and civic-minded human being, guided by love and reason.

When we look at the cultural, political, social, and individual situation, however, things seem to be rather different. Individually and collectively we find corruption, perversion—"*homo homini lupus*." Many sufferings of the human race are caused by nature—like diseases and death—but many more are the result of human beings hurting, torturing, and killing each other. We usually try very hard to suppress and forget this demonic side, but we are usually not successful. Even more perplexing, if somebody is successful in completely splitting off or apparently eliminating his or her dark side, he or she becomes empty, bloodless, and—in the end—not connected to any kind of eros.

It is certainly very important to fight day and night for morality and decency. But at the same time it is just as important to stay continually in touch with what Moore calls dark eros, our dark side.

In this endeavor, as Moore shows us, the writings of the Marquis de Sade are of extreme importance. Through his sexual mythology de Sade shows us our demonic potential.

Sexuality is the raw material of one of the most potent mythologies of today. Individual and collective sexual fantasies depict in a symbolic way the human psyche. Ancient mythologies of Gods, etc., have somehow lost their significance as symbolical representations of the human psyche. In sexual fantasies, however, the mythology of the human soul is very much alive and touches both soul and body.

The Marquis de Sade has created a fascinating mythology of our dark side. His figures—his men and women, his innocent girls and debauched libertines—are not representations of actual human beings, but purely symbolic mythological images of parts of our psyche. So, it's very difficult to read de Sade and be really touched by his bizarre fantasies, touched in a way that we realize he is writing about human life, about us.

Now here Thomas Moore has done a marvelous job. He more or less systematically takes up all the sexual images which de Sade presents and translates them so that we can understand them as part of our own shadow, as part of our dark eros, which even if repugnant and frightening have yet always to be looked at and without whom we lose all strength and depth.

Just to take an easy example, in de Sade's novel *Justine and Juliette* Justine is a charming, beautiful, innocent girl, who is ravished, raped, tortured, degraded, etc., by the ruthless libertines. Here, the sexual imagination symbolically represents the necessary ravishing of the innocent pure part of our soul. Innocence is in the final analysis a refusal to come really in touch with this world. The innocent soul has to be initiated and forced into the dark and fascinating reality of life. If the soul remains innocent, it is not really becoming human but is just like a plant.

Or, to take another example, bondage and bonds play a big role in sadistic fantasies and in the work of the Marquis de Sade. But we all are in bondage to life, obligations, passions, enthusiasms. Whenever we are alive and committed to something, we are at the same time bound, in some way helplessly tied, not at all free in the naive image of a free and independent human being.

Thomas Moore makes it possible to fully appreciate the Marquis de Sade as a teacher of our dark eros, of our darkly frightening, demonic side. To use a standard phrase, Moore's book should be a "must" for everybody even only vaguely interested in psychology, in the soul, but especially a "must" for every member of the helping professions. Peculiarly enough, we in the helping professions are especially inclined to ignore dark eros, although it is part of the motivation for our work. For instance, psychotherapy has a very sadistic side: we have to coolly and objectively analyze the patient in order to help him. If we approach him only with sentimental compassion, we just fall for all the tricks of his neurosis and can never really be of any help.

I have, however, one reservation concerning the work of the Marquis de Sade which perhaps Thomas Moore shares less. Although polytheism is mentioned very often in Moore's book, I have the impression that de Sade is an extreme monotheist and therefore any kind of tragic conflict is completely missing in his writings. The symbolic persons he has created are absolutely straight; they are purists or puritans. Their one aim and one pleasure is to invert the standard collective values. They know without a doubt what they want and in what they delight. But the so-called Sadeian culture is only meaningful if the other side—the white eros, so to speak—is taken into account, too. Because the real difficulty of our lives lies in our uninterruptedly tragic situation: nothing is clear, everything is ambivalent, we are always torn between heaven and hell, between the devil and Christ—to put it very simply. The genius of the Marquis de Sade was to show us dark eros through sexual images, but this genius was not sufficient to show us the whole range of our life, the suffering of our tragic conflicts.

I missed something else, too, in Thomas Moore's book—namely, a hint of an understanding of why we have good reasons to repress consciously our dark eros, our sadistic side. The way we humans treat each other is very often not dominated by our morality and decency but much more by our sadism, which is apparent not only in individual lives but especially in collective events. In World War I twenty million young men died. In World War II the German Nazis coolly exterminated six million Jews, Stalin later liquidated twenty million Russians, Mao Tse-tung forty million Chinese, and Pol Pot a third of the population of Cambodia. Today we experience the murderous civil war in Yugoslavia and read with horror that in Rwanda a million people have been literally slaughtered within a few months. Teenage boys have cut apart little children with machetes, and soldiers have stopped massacring people only because they became too exhausted to continue. Dark eros is no joke: we must be wary of it. The distance between feeling and acting out is often very short, whether these fantasies be conscious or repressed. How close our dark eros is even in fairly peaceful countries shows in our fascination with horror stories, tales of murders, rapes, accidents, etc., which are practically the basis for all tabloids.

I am indeed very thankful to the Marquis de Sade and especially to Thomas Moore's book *Dark Eros*. Moore brings de Sade nearer to us, explains him to us, and makes it possible to deal with our own dark eros in an unmoralistic way. But in making the Marquis more understandable and even in some way being enthusiastic about his works, Moore might have neglected somewhat the real horror of our lived-out shadow. It's quite repulsive and disgusting to read how de Sade is interested in the taste of our feces and imagines himself their connoisseur; it's frightening to read in de Sade how women are tortured with delight. But these matters are still nothing compared with the endless horrible slaughtering and torturing which characterize all of human history.

Having said that, I would like to finish by saying that I am very impressed by the courage of Thomas Moore. Psychological and moral courage is required for writing so precisely and deeply about the works of the Marquis de Sade. Moore's book is indeed a truly moral work.

ADOLF GUGGENBÜHL-CRAIG

Acknowledgments

I first received encouragement to write this book over ten years ago from Rafael López-Pedraza. His appreciation for the psychology and aesthetics of the grotesque has kept me on track as I have struggled to find necessity and beauty in Sade's fiction. I am also indebted to James Hillman, Patricia Berry, and William Burford for their suggestions in the early phases of the writing, and more recently to Christopher Bamford, Pat Toomay, and Angelyn Spignesi. I would also like to thank Mary Helen Sullivan for editing the manuscript with a light but penetrating touch.

1.

Novelist, Pervert, Doctor of the Soul

Exactly two hundred years ago the Marquis de Sade sat in his dirty, rat-infested cell in the Bastille, cursing his fate and yet remaining loyal to his odd way of looking at human nature. The American War of Independence was just ending, and the French Revolution was warming up. Sade's time was an age of reason, we say, a time when the universe seemed knowable and when it was compared to a clock in its mechanical precision. His was also a time when the wealthy strutted their affectations and quests for pleasure publicly and when the hypocrisy of public values rendered social justice arbitrary and capricious. In other words, it was a time much like ours.

Although Sade spent a good portion of his life in detention, his biography reads like an adventure story: educated by a cleric uncle, well positioned in the military, falling in love with actresses, loved and hated by his mother-in-law, escaping from prison with his valet, pursued by an indefatigable Inspector Maurais, released in revolution to serve as magistrate, becoming fat and bloated in an asylum cell shared at times with a young woman, watching from his window as his compatriots were hanged. In the midst of this adventurous and distressing life, he wrote novels, plays, and essays that carry an exceedingly dark point of view rarely equaled in literature.

One has the impression from his biography and from his fate in the history of literature that Sade's way is so remarkably alien to accepted values that during his lifetime and into the present he has been made into a figure of myth, of grand proportions and of completely evil cast. In effect, he was never liberated from his prison cell. He died imprisoned at Charenton, but still he is locked in the back wards of literature, history, and common opinion. His works are securely fixed on lists of forbidden books. In some bookstores even today you have to venture into a curtained adult book section if you want to find one of his novels or even a biography or criticism. In one library I was escorted to a padlocked basement room and given an hour to riffle through some pages of Sade criticism. In a biographical catalogue in the field of arts and letters, in which figures are identified as artist, writer, painter, philosopher, and so on, I found Sade labeled simply "French pervert."

Critics have also found perversity in his writing style. He is often accused of being monotonous, undescriptive, repetitious, rambling, and dull. Some modern editions intentionally skip over the dull parts and reduce thousands of pages of fiction to a few hundred. Sade not only makes life appear ugly, he does so in an ugly manner. Any positive appraisal of Sade has to inquire into his unusual aesthetic. The twistedness of his ideas seems to call for a special form of presentation.

Although Sade's images are outrageously obscene, they are echoed on almost every page of the daily newspaper where one can read in detail about murder, accident, corruption, competition, plotting, deception, and extreme ethical insensitivity. Sade seems to have fixed his vision on this underworld with the tenacity and intensity you might find in mystical literature. He approaches humankind's love of evil with the devotion and faithfulness of a saint, and so with good reason he has been called "The Divine Marquis."

Sade has had his champions and disciples; among them are Swinburne, Apollinaire, Oscar Wilde, Andre Breton, and Georges Bataille. He has been praised as a cataloguer of mankind's perversity and has been seen as a forerunner of Freud, himself a member of the fraternity of uglifiers. In his extraordinary book *Sade, Fourier, Loyola*, Roland Barthes has penetrated into the deeper metaphoric nature of Sade's language and imagery, comparing his vision to the spirit of utopianism and of monastic life. While some modern critics examine subtle literary elements in Sade's writing, Barthes's work cuts through the literal viewpoint usually brought to Sade, seeing life patterns and structures in his fictive ceremonies and therefore hinting at the potential archetypal dimension of his imagination.

While I engage in an extensive archetypal analysis of Sade's fiction, I do not want to overlook popular opinion. Sade *is* perverse. He *is* a figure of mythic proportions, and that dimension, too, should be investigated. If we approach Sade's writing as we would Greek mythology, we might understand better the bare skeletons of his scenarios and avoid personalistic interpretations of his ugly characters. As many commentators have pointed out, Sade's fictional scenes are often physically impossible to perform in actual life, and at the very least they are completely outrageous. Like the ancient mythographers, he uses grand strokes to paint the perverted universe that charmed him, and so he could be read as a conduit of an underworld mythology, like Homer, rather than as a social critic using fiction to espouse his personal convictions.

In his essay "Reflections on the Novel," he makes his own case for the strange slant of his writing:

> It is Nature that has to be grasped when one works in the area of fiction. It is mankind's heart, the most remarkable of Nature's works, and not virtue, because virtue, however lovely and necessary, is only one facet of this extraordinary heart, the profound study of which is essential to the novelist. And the novel, the faithful mirror of this heart, has to explore its every fold.[1]

This passage makes it clear that Sade, for his part, saw his fiction as a bitterly honest exploration of the soul. Take away virtue, give up the effort to present the soul in its best light or with motives of inspiration or self-improvement, and what do you find? Sade finds a black hole. He comes up against psychological anti-matter, a complete inversion of societal interpretations and values.

He had read Jean-Jacques Rousseau, the philosopher of bountiful nature, who was twenty-eight years his senior, and he was impressed with the variety of ways in which nature expresses herself in the customs of peoples around the world. If nature sanctions a certain human behavior in any society whatsoever, Sade implies, that is evidence of the necessity and value of that behavior. This argument, which Sade presents time after time as an anthropological excursion within a tale, is similar to archetypal theories which use the universality of an image or theme as evidence of its profound necessity. It might be helpful in reading Sade to translate "Nature" as "archetype," to understand that he is trying to show that certain themes which on the surface we find repugnant from a deeper point of view have their place. It is up to us, therefore, not to moralize against them because they do not fit into our limited repertoire of acceptable human actions, but to contemplate their necessity.

Sade also confessed the demands he felt in his own nature. In a letter written to his wife from prison he says:

> You say that my way of thinking cannot be tolerated? What of it? The man who alters his way of thinking to suit others is a fool. My way of thinking is the result of my reflections. It is part of my inner being, the way I am made. I do not contradict them, and would not even if I wished to. For my system, which you disapprove of, is also my greatest comfort in life, the source of all my happiness—it means more to me than my life itself.[2]

This passionate letter expressing faithfulness to his own given, inner vision hints at the power of the dark muse that took his creative gifts in hand. He wrote daimonically, not only demonically. Apparently he was as much taken over by this underworld genius as is a poet who surrenders to the love sonnet. He was held to that peculiar perverse angle and vision and honored it to the point of giving up most of his freedoms on its behalf. This is not to say that he remained imprisoned without complaint. His letters are horrific cries for freedom and pleas for minor comforts. But even from prison he refuses to betray his dark, divine obsession.

Sade the man, therefore, embodies the personality of this underworld we will explore through his fiction. It is easier, of course, to take our models and guides from among the virtuous of history. Not many would profess a Hitler or Bluebeard as their inspiring genius. But in order to fathom the undeniable tendencies of the soul toward the outrageously dark, we may need an idol like Sade. Could it be that the mythologization of Sade himself is part of an attempt to find an inner figure adequate to evil, someone aligned with the brutalities and odd loves of the soul? No doubt it is easy to suppress this figure, since he is so repugnant to other, more familiar points of view and since he is so far from our professed ideals. But we might remember Sade's repeated principle and apply it to ourselves: if nature plants "sick" fantasies in our imaginations, then perhaps nature is expressing an unfathomable and revolting truth.

The Sadeian Soul

My interest in Sade became serious shortly after I began practicing psychotherapy. Well-intentioned, upright, high-minded people would present dreams and fantasies filled with exquisite torture, murder, sexual perversion, and graphic scatology. They were disturbed by these dreams and assumed that they hinted at horrible repressed wishes or character disorders. But I had been prepared by my studies in archetypal psychology to understand the pathology in images as a genre of expression. So, I thought, if I do not moralize these dreams, then I need help approaching their imagery on its own terms. I need a guide who is consonant with their strange mystery rather than one who is moralistic and insensitive to their necessity. I sought out a specialist of this particular kind of imagination, and I was surprised to find the detail, the consistency, and the honesty of Sade's fiction. If C. G. Jung resorts to imagery of the Old Testament to "amplify" a religious dream, then I could turn to Sade to intensify my appreciation of images from the outskirts of sexuality and the dregs of human behavior.

If, when working with images, we are to "dream the dream onward"—according to Jung's rule of thumb—then to dream a scatological dream onward entails finding further imagery in the genre and mood. If we follow James Hillman's dictum that we should stay close to the given image, then we need a point of comparison that does not entice us away from the repugnant violence and nausea at the heart of many images. We need a Sade as much as we need a Hesiod, who describes among other things the castration of a father by a son, to remind us of the place of certain strains in nature that affront decency.

The tone around Sade's books and around his persona *should be* dark and unacceptable. Maybe it would be a mistake to take the locks off the library rooms where his writing is sequestered. If we clean him up with psychological jargon and therapeutic intentions, we will have lost his guidance. The foul atmosphere that surrounds him is like the sulfuric stench of the devil. It would be a travesty of hell to smell roses when Satan appears. My purpose, then, in turning to Sade is to find a darkening of consciousness, to seek out a foul-smelling imagery appropriate for the amplification of those dreams and fantasies and art pieces that reveal an underworld aesthetic and a shadowy psychological reality.

One of the most important moves in psychotherapy is to take whatever is presented and simply hold it and give it a place. A great deal of the trouble one hears in therapy has more to do with fighting what is given than with the given thing itself. Here Sade offers help. If we start out agreeing with him that these horrifying images of the soul have a special necessity, that they are simply givens of nature, then we might better hold on to similar imagery that appears in life and in dreams.

Sade, in his perversity, helps us fend off temptations toward moralism. Donning his perverse attitude, we might even appreciate some of the otherwise objectionable images that occur to everyone and that in at least subtle ways give a sharp black tone even to ordinary life.

Sadeian imagery, defined by misfortune, violence, evil intention, perversion, and self-serving manipulation, occurs in unexpected places. Fairy tales and children's stories tell of atrocities to children and families. Parents are harsh, a wolf dresses up like Grandmother and threatens to eat a child, babies fall from the tops of trees, children die in lands of enchantment. Not surprisingly, the child who is yet some distance from the moral values of society enjoys his Sadeian pleasures, like telling gruesome and sickening stories, torturing animals, toying with feces, playing doctor, and waging wars. Some argue that these traditional Sadeian themes in children's literature are dangerous and harmful. Taking Sade seriously, however, suggests that the soul is nourished by images that reflect the less than virtuous side of life.

Moving toward an appreciation of the "perverted image," we may begin with a distinction that is frequently made about film and literature and yet is not applied sufficiently to Sade. Atrocious acts in fiction are not of the same order as atrocious acts in life. A novel is not a chronicle. A page from Sade may not be autobiographical in the literal sense. To imagine ugliness is not the same as perpetrating it. The fictive nature of Sade's work, especially its mythic dimensions, suggests a distinction between "sadistic" acts and the "Sadeian" imagination. The Sadeian image may be a "natural" expression of the psyche, while the sadistic act might be a return of the repressed image in actual life. Unless we make this distinction carefully, we will be arguing against the perversity of image out of our outrage over sadistic acts.

Of course, it is not possible to draw clear boundaries between imagination and life. Imagination is always liminal, with a part in mind and a part in body, as Renaissance writers often said. Sade's admitted taste for libertinage in his life cannot be completely separated from his fiction. Where does the life-imagination split from the art-imagination? And what about Sadeianism today? When a couple engages in sado-masochistic activity, is this fiction or actual brutality? Are these rites of healing, or are they literally destructive and harmful? Can a person be led to violence by reading about it? Or is he purged of his violent capacities by entertaining imagery that keeps his tendencies in the realm of fiction?

As we enter the fictive world of Sade, we will often be aware that we are walking this thin line. But that is the beauty and the terror of literature: to take us to that edge where categories fail and certainty retires. How else could literature effect its catharsis? Placed in the midst of revolting imagination, we feel, touch, taste, and smell the atmosphere of this corner of the soul. For catharsis it is as necessary to feel the revulsion in Sade as it is to sense the rhythm in Dylan Thomas and the meter in Shakespeare. The medium, in this case a particularly foul one, is an integral part of the message.

A Sadeian Psychology

James Hillman has written extensively about the importance of the "pathologizing" nature of the soul. Perhaps, he says, our own pathologies are what make us individuals. We all deviate from the normal. We all suffer pathology. The pathologies of the soul also tear us away from the ego, from heroic fantasies, from attachment to life, from our narrowly conceived hopes and affections. In a word, pathology is iconoclastic. Sade, of course, is an extravagant iconoclast. Every line of his fiction shatters an accepted and familiar truth and violates a tender moral loyalty. The repugnance we feel when we read a passage from *Justine* is the clash of our own cultivated morality with a contradictory value from Sade.

The mythology of Sade can be seen, therefore, as a particular instance of the pathologizing need of the soul. Sade challenges our usual values, often confined by the limited perimeters of consciousness and the easy heroics of ordinary virtue, inviting us to consider some shady alternatives. In this he serves the soul rather than the ego. He speaks for hidden and repressed mystery over against known and tested mores of civilization, another reason to refer to him as "The Divine Marquis." His God is dark, his theology twisted, and yet he opens a great, rusty door that leads down into a pit where the soul's basement delights are to be found.

Therefore Sade extends psychological space, another advantage in Hillman's analysis of pathologizing. Architecture and place, we will see in some detail, are important in Sade's fiction. We feel resistance to entering that malodorous arena where preposterous events take place; nevertheless, Sade's presentation of that neglected space invites us to explore new territory and to find that the soul has more capacity than heretofore suspected. Sade's brotherhood with Freud consists not only in their attraction to the perverse but also in their psychological viewpoint. Sade the psychologist serves the soul by allowing it to embrace more and repress less.

Again Hillman's analysis of pathology links it directly to myth. Pathology, in life and in image, forces us to look behind the facade of natural events to their mythic dimensions. If they are taken at a naive, literal level, Sade's stories simply repel. But if they are allowed to stir imagination, they unveil a world of myth where disaster and grotesque fantasy are the norm. Comparing Sade's fiction to mythology, as I intend to do while examining specific themes in his writing, one sees many parallels. For the Gods and Goddesses of Greek mythology, incest, parricide, theft, mass murder, clever sexual connections, and exotic ceremonies are the order of the day. The comparisons to Sade are so striking that one is led more to consider Sade as mythological than mythology as Sadeian, although both are true.

Rafael López-Pedraza, the archetypal psychologist and mythologist who has written insightfully of the grotesque, also invites a psychological reading of Sade. "I would like to see the images of sado-masochism," he writes in *Hermes and His Children*, "as having archetypal roots in humankind, and as offering a spectrum that can be viewed in psychotherapy as the demand of a part of nature in *need* of being lived."[3] Again, he suggests necessity. The mythology of sado-masochistic themes has a place in life and in the structure of the soul.

This is a key for reading Sade: not to look at literal behavior, which clearly will be entirely repugnant, but to see this mythology as an essential ingredient of the soul's nature. Then we have to ask questions full of poetic resonance. Why is the soul's innocence tortured? Why is Sade so murderous toward parents? What is the nature of his attacks on Christianity? What is his fascination for the sexual organs and for sex without love? If we take Sade's writing as a program for social experimentation, we will reduce him to absurdity. But if we take him as an iconoclast of fantasy, then we may want to re-examine many of our assumptions about family and sex. As odd as it may seem, Pedraza's recommendation is right on the mark: the deep fantasies in sado-masochism need to be lived.

Defensive Morality

What we often call morality is in fact defense. Morality of depth involves a slowly developing entry into some fundamental mystery that challenges human life. Decision regarding action and behavior reveals itself gradually. This morality is complex, full of the shadows of uncertainty; and yet, if taken deep enough, it offers sufficient moral confidence to do anything with courage. Deep morality and courage are reciprocal; they require each other. Deep morality can never be separated from imagination: it is one of its functions. Our moral dilemmas demand that we explore life and soul with full imaginative power, in order to get close to the mysteries that give life its verticality, its sacredness, meaning, and value.

Since morality with depth demands so much, we are often satisfied with substitutes: moral codes taken literally or moral convictions and stands narrowly defined. This thin morality, without imagination, defends against the challenge of all that is not understood and cannot be categorized. The code says: honor thy father and thy mother. But dream and fantasy sometimes say: kill your parents, get away from them. Some dreams seem to imitate rites of passage in which death, blood, and violence are symbols in initiation. But dreams and rites are not literal actions. A person can love his actual parents and yet find in his fantasy a rejection of the parental figure. Through an image of murder, the archetypal parent is transformed and identity with child consciousness shifted.

In reading Sade we have two options. We can approach him with superficial and literalistic moral positions and find him infinitely wanting. Or, we can let him lead us into a more subtle moral sensitivity. The only morality adequate to the complexities of life is one that has been sculpted in the presence of the shadow. If Sade's fiction is abrasive to the reader's moral positions, then that rub may be exactly what is needed to deepen the moral imagination.

Another moral issue in Sade has to do with what James Hillman has called "psychological polytheism." It is not necessary, in order to read Sade open-mindedly, to become a Sadeianite. You do not have to give everything over to Sade. Jung describes polytheism as an alchemical journey through the stars. Reading Sade is like stopping at one of the planets to pick up another dimension of the soul's character. Sade's world is one among many. It is possible to appreciate Sade's hatred of Venus and then go on to the planet of Venus and enjoy her comforts.

Not all dreams are scatological. This is only one station of the soul, albeit an important and essential one. Something mysterious and meaningful is going on when Jung dreams of God's gigantic turd and sees it as a revelation, when a sincere person dreams of overflowing toilets in a particularly initiatory time of life, when language is colored with scatological expletives, and when in mythology the Goddess of beauty is born from the castration of her father. These Sadeian events hint at a blue velvet fabric in the soul's make-up. If we turn our heads in revulsion at the sight of these Sadeian elements, we may be missing out on an essential part of the mystery—thus the value of his imagination and the many thousands of pages of Sade's writing.

The "Sadeian Imagination," a viewpoint from which we can see certain strong shadows in life and soul, can be gleaned from Sade's massive volumes of fiction. But this imagination itself stands apart from the literal Sade. Consisting in a general appreciation for the necessity of evil, it sees through the personal level in literature to dark mythic themes which perversely nourish the soul. It sees through the literal evils of life to the necessities that are actually destructive only when repressed and literalized. Whatever Sade loves can be taken as necessary and even valuable from this particular oblique angle on the psyche. Without the Sadeian imagination, we give our attention to attacking perceived evils. But as long as our only response is moralistic judgment, there is no hope for psychological insight or, more importantly, for the recovery of soul so solidly repressed by moralism.

Sade's libertines enjoy the pleasures of their underground activities. They experience true joy, even though the cause of their joy looks repugnant. The absolute delight so often expressed by the libertines suggests that the soul finds satisfaction in the evils Sade presents in his mythology. From our customary upperworld moral point of view, it is difficult to understand how libertine pleasures could have anything to do with genuine psychological fulfillment. But, once Sade is seen as a mythographer rather than a straight philosopher, when the reader appreciates the strong irony and dark humor that color every page, then it is possible to recognize the validity of a libertine psychology that reveals the strange but undeniable loves and inverted inclinations of the psyche.

2.

Love's Inversions

Love, as we usually understand it, is not to be found much in Sade's fiction, unless it is being ridiculed, satirized, or used to intensify the outrageousness of some atrocity. Yet, in another sense, every page of Sade is about love, a strange sort of love that is signaled by strong sexual responses and elaborate rituals aimed at securing the highest pleasures. The very heart of Sade's fictional enterprise is an exploration of the erotic, but it is a dark eros that fascinates him. The erotic in Sade takes many odd forms: desire and longing for violence, delight in misfortune, fascination with unusual aspects of the body, pleasure in rites of dominance and submission, delicious sacrilege, the love of caprice over principle, and disgusting taste in food and manners.

Modern psychology uses words like *compulsion* and *obsession* to describe actual cases of extreme attachment to a symptom. Sade's mythological stories show the deep fantasies within compulsions, but they root all of these experiences in desire. At first it may seem odd to claim that the sickening and frightening issues Sade presents have anything to do with desire, but that is the value of his approach—to unveil the stirrings of love in places that seem void of it. From the outside, for example, a person's failure to overcome compulsive smoking might look like failure of will, but from the Sadeian inside what is revealed is the strength of a love—something loves the smoke—that is objectionable to the ego but not to the soul.

Interest in misfortune is not altogether foreign to us. On the highway, traffic comes to a crawl as drivers otherwise in a hurry slow down to gape at an accident. Is this merely idle curiosity, or is it a deeper interest in accident and misfortune? Isn't there desire in that glance from the car window, a hunger to see the destructive hand of fate? Aren't we attracted by the pathologies of everyday life?

The word *accident* is from *casus*, "fall." It echoes the great fall of Adam and Eve and suggests failure, the fall from grace and perfection. It is related to *cadence*, an ending, which in music and poetry has an important and satisfying aesthetic function. It is also connected to *chance*, the fall of the dice. All these senses of *accident* are at work when we pass an overturned truck on the road and can't help twisting our necks to catch sight of this common portion of human life. Perhaps ultimately we are attracted to misfortune because it is a figuration of Death, whom we usually deny and yet with whom we have an intimate relationship.

In *Philosophy in the Bedroom* Sade writes: "Destruction being one of the chief laws of Nature, nothing that destroys can be criminal." (238) Not only does the repressed return in symptoms and fruitless behavior, it also becomes an object of desire. If we repress the law that Sade speaks for—nature's way of destruction—we are drawn back to that law when we see evidence of it. We are curious about its meaning and its unavoidable place in life. Therefore the gapers' road jam, the fascination for misfortune in soap operas and tabloids, and even the draw of calamity in high art, as in Hamlet's grand depression, hide as they reveal our natural love for the destructive side of life.

Though love sometimes takes the soft forms of interest and fascination, it can be more overt. A couple goes to a therapist to complain about their sex life. A few months ago they decided to spice up their sex by adding some sado-masochistic play, purely for the fun of it. The woman wanted her husband to tie her to the bed and lightly slap her. The man wanted some humiliation and playful beating for himself. Soon the rites lost their playfulness. Something demonic in each of them broke through so that the beating was no longer subtle, the dominance no longer mutual, the humiliation now too painful to bear. They are confused, embarrassed, and frightened by their desire for violence. They had no idea it had such deep and strong roots. Now they are afraid of what they have unleashed.

Desire takes the form of sexual response. Eros puts on his uniform of sexuality to give desire some ritualistic and symbolic play. But it is not always easy to appreciate the power and depth of desire. This couple had obviously remained at some distance from their darker longings. When they decided to let their fantasies enter life in a safe and harmless way, they thought they could be in charge. They were surprised to discover the power of desire to subdue reason and ego. Once released, like a genie from a bottle, Eros took over, and they were led to explore issues of power, dominance, and violence as neglected ingredients in their marriage.

Love and marriage go together like a horse and carriage, the old song says. In relation to marriage, love is usually assumed to mean care, sharing, affection—all positive feelings. When marriage breaks out into argument, beating, and divorce, we see these developments as a failure of love, as something contrary to the marriage vows. But Sade offers a different idea. In his view nature has a more comprehensive desire. Argument, separation, power, selfishness—these are also legitimate objects of desire. Just because they are denied does not mean they do not have a right to exist. Not admitting to this "negative" side of desire, we are surprised when it appears and assume it to be the eruption of some completely alien evil. It is not necessary to read Sade as inviting the literal acting out of that evil, but simply the admission that selfishness and the desire for violence and misfortune do in fact appear in the hearts of the best of us. One might imagine a Sadeian marriage in which the more difficult loves of the soul are invited and accepted. In *Juliette* Sade recommends that a woman bring to a man such "virtues" as lust, greed, deceit, infidelity, and hypocrisy. He adds to the list an admonition against pregnancy which "spoils the figure, endangers the health, and is bad from every point of view." (435) The very things we consider most valuable in relationship Sade criticizes. Those things we try to avoid in the name of virtue Sade recommends.

Sade gives voice to the shadows of love. The society he creates in his fiction, the lords and chattels of libertinage are the precise figures we deny, repress, ignore, and undervalue in our sentimental view of morals and social structure. But he teaches his characters and his readers that they can learn to love this underworld. The pedantic tone in his novels is not plain persuasion toward an actual life of moral abandon; it is a recognition of feelings and thoughts that already exist in the heart and in behavior. We do lust, we do dissemble, we do flatter for our own purposes. Denial of these loves leads to a sentimentalized world, a split life weighty with the burden of maintaining impossible ideals and foiled with the incursion of repressed shadow appearing again and again as personal symptom and social disaster. The key into Sade is a slight twist of imagination, the decision that the frenzied pursuit of right living, impossible virtues, and sentimental values is neither necessary nor an honest reflection of how we live even in the midst of those ideals.

Eros the Prick

The following is another passage from *Juliette*. in which a young woman is learning to become a Sadeian officer. Juliette is talking with her tutor, Saint-Fond, a name that suggests low-life or the Underworld. They are appraising a girl named Palmire:

> "Palmire is an orphan. She comes of a good line, and has no parents except an elderly aunt who gave me an excellent portrait of the girl."
>
> "So you love her, Juliette?"
>
> "Saint-Fond, I don't love anything. I am moved by caprice only."
>
> "I feel this pretty creature lacks absolutely nothing of what is needed to make a delicious victim; undeniably she is beautiful, it is quite certain she would be yet more so in distress, she has magnificent hair, a sublime ass whose qualities are indeed outstanding. . . . Here, Juliette, see how my prick soars at the thought of martyrizing her." (346)

Palmire, being an orphan, of a good line, and with excellent references, is a prime candidate for victimizing. The libertine loves innocence. His mission in life is to spoil what innocence he finds. But he does not love innocent love. Juliette proves her worth to the libertine life by acknowledging that she doesn't love in the sentimental sense. Erotic motivation for her is caprice, based on chance and not relationship. It is light, impersonal, and short on social value. She is learning a truth which Sade's readers might seriously consider, that there is a kind of love not rooted in relationship. It is unstable and unreliable and yet love all the same. This light love is the Sadeian shadow to any insistence that love must always be profound and lasting. From the Sadeian point of view, a passing romance, a brief affair, or an attraction that has no substance to it, no possibility for "relationship," has a place among the shadow necessities of the psyche.

Saint-Fond then notices that part of Palmire's body especially honored by Sade's libertines, the backside. Later we will explore the Sadeian body and its peculiar erogenous zones, including this beloved part. The libertine is interested in the backside of innocence, and if Saint-Fond makes a quick move from the girl's virtues to her bottom, that is the way of Sade. His erotic attachments invert whatever is placed before him. For Sade the bottom always has priority and presides, so to speak, at the top.

From Saint-Fond's soaring prick we know that eros has been summoned by thoughts of victimization and the sight of the backside. The sure indication that a certain behavior is Sadeian is eros erect, the penis upright. This is not merely a pornographic element in Sade; it is another version of ithyphallic images found in religious sanctuaries around the world. Sexual response is the objective correlative of interested desire. That soaring prick indicates a context that is specifically Sadeian. What does not arouse the phallus belongs to some other universe.

If Christ's cross can be interpreted as the grand climax of his religion,[1] or if we follow Leo Steinberg's thesis that Christian iconography often shows Jesus with a thinly veiled erection, symbolizing the resurrection,[2] then similarly we might see the phallic response of the libertine as an image of fulfillment, pointing to various acts which satisfy Sadeian desire. It would be literalistic merely to find pornography in the ithyphallic images in Sade's stories. The erection is always clearly in a context carefully elaborated by the libertine.

The presence of the phallus image throughout the world's religions and the role of sex in religious iconography give a strong imagistic context to Sade's depiction of eros. Two centuries after Sade we tend to limit eros to sex, pornography, or at best the dynamics of interpersonal relationships. But it might help in reading Sade psychologically to recall the much broader conception of eros in the Western tradition.

In *Theogony*, the early Greek poet Hesiod describes the origin of things according to archaic belief. In the beginning there came forth Chaos, then Gaia the Earth Goddess, then Tartaros in the pit of the earth, and finally Eros, "who is love, handsomest among all the immortals, who breaks the limbs' strength, who in all gods, in all human beings overpowers the intelligence in the breast, and all their shrewd planning."[3] Eros breaks the strength to act and the capacity to think. We could imagine eros bending the power of other eternal factors in life as well: the need for survival, the planned life, hope for success, family loyalties, moral sensitivities, and religious convictions. The erotic is a powerful force that stretches the moral world we have in place, if it does not completely break it apart.

Hesiod's eros is primordial, suggesting that whenever we are in the realm of the erotic we are close to foundations.

Becoming attracted to a person, idea, or thing is never simple or superficial. All issues of love, however slight and passing, intimate ultimate concerns. Love is always in touch with the core of being.

In the evolution of the Gods, Eros follows Chaos, a gap or yawn, an opening in life in which Eros can appear and do his work. Eros is ever near his source in chaos and so threatens order and structure. This sibling origin of eros and chaos pictures the vast crater that eros can blast when he appears unexpectedly at the center of an ordered life. What is more unsettling than an unsought fall into love? Along with it may come powerful fantasies in which cherished relationships fall apart, or a career collapses, or long-held values crumble. The close relation of eros to chaos also implies a new order, and ordering life anew is one of Sade's primary preoccupations.

The Orphic sect in Greek religion gave eros an even more powerful role in the workings of things. The Orphic Eros is a God who can bring worlds into existence. He is cosmogonic, a world-maker. The classic source for the image of Eros as a maker of worlds is Aristophanes' *The Birds*:

> Then in the infinite bosom of Erebos first of all black-winged Night bore a wind-sown egg, from which in the circling of seasons came Eros the much desired, his back gleaming with twin golden wings, swift as the whirling clouds. He mingling in broad Tartaros with winged and gloomy chaos hatched out our race, and brought us first to see the light. Before that there was no race of the immortals, until Eros mingled all things together. Then from their mingling with each other was born Heaven and Ocean and Earth and the deathless race of the blessed gods.[4]

In both of these Greek sources Eros is allied with dark, negative powers: chaos, night, and Tartaros—the vast emptiness at the bottom of the world. A gloomy place through which souls pass on their way to Hades, Erebos is where Eros is born. Erotic experience originates in this gloomy place of the soul. These classical passages suggest that Sade's dark eros is not unprecedented in sublime sacred literature. Even in these early sources erotic experience has a disturbing relation to the underworld.

Love cannot be explained by surface causes. A lover says, "I fell in love with her because she had a curl over her eye when she waited on me in the drugstore." Another says, in Sadeian fashion, "I liked her ass." A woman whose lengthy marriage has ended because of a new love in her life confesses: "I didn't want this. I expected to be true to my family for the rest of my life, and then this young man rang my doorbell by mistake." He may have just arrived from Hades.

Marriages may be made in heaven, but they are hatched in hell. Even though we go to great lengths to keep it positive, love contains a strong element of negativity and emptiness. In a famous passage in Plato's *Symposium*, love is seen as the offspring of Plenty and Want. There is plenty of feeling and fantasy in love, but there are also strong need and emptiness. Although love can be creative, it is also destructive and entropic. If most literature focuses on the pleasures and pains of love, Sade turns our attention to its dark objects.

Eros is also wind-sown. Having golden wings, he is compared to the whirling clouds that take many shapes but are always turning and drifting. In art Eros is shown with impressive wings, as an angel or a spirit. He blows in and out of life, as though on the wind, as though he *were* a wind. The Greeks sometimes called him a daimon, neither God nor human, an ambassador between the two realms, a metaxy, a go-between.

To be caught up in Eros is to be taken somewhere. Not a static condition, being in love is to be on the way, in transit. Love not only transforms, it also translates, transports, and transposes. When psychology speaks of love as transference, it captures the tendency of love to keep things in motion and unstable. Sade's interesting focus on caprice—he wrote a whole play on the theme—draws attention to love's unpredictable moves, so obvious in life but easy to dismiss as an aberration rather than as an essential property.

The Orphic hymn emphasizes the duty of Eros to "mingle." He mingles the sexes and all parts of the world, keeping the planets in orbit and the seasons in cycle. Ultimately he is responsible for the cosmos. *Cosmos* means "ornament." A cosmos is an ordered and ornamented world, one that has its own logic and appeal. What we love, what appeals to us, shapes the world we live in. Erotic stirrings, even when they seem small and petty, can render a new cosmos, a world defined by a new aesthetic and a new scheme of meaning. If the soul is polytheistic, we always live in many worlds in various stages of becoming and dying. The fantasies that rush in at moments of intense love are the raw materials for a new construction, a new way of imagining and participating in life.

Young Eros, often pictured as a child or adolescent, not only makes new worlds, he makes life feel new. He rejuvenates. The lover feels the adolescence of Eros in his body and in the excitation of fantasy. Personally Sade comes across as an incorrigible rebel. His mother-in-law, who used all her political connections to keep Sade in prison for many years, claimed over and over that he could not be trusted to behave properly.

He was clearly more an embarrassment than a threat. Even the officials who held the key to his cell knew that his actual offenses were adolescent foolishness and not the serious crimes depicted in his writing.

When Sade was forty-three and in prison, his wife wrote a letter to the King of Sardinia pleading for her husband's freedom. "My husband is not to be classed with the rogues of whom the universe should be purged. An excess of fantasy, Sir, resulted in a sort of misdemeanor . . . because of a youthful folly which endangered no life."[5] Sade's letters do reveal an "excess of fantasy," an imagination fueled by erotic exploration and wildly faithful, with an unbounded adolescent fervor, to the unusual directions of his curiosity.

In Sade's fiction eros is the ordering factor that determines various details of ritual, crime, and sexual arrangements. The erotic response of the libertine charts the contours of his sexual universe. The libertine is the persona or face of this special world. What he, or occasionally she, likes is what fits into this "turned around" or perverted cosmos. In Greek and Roman mythology, Eros is a young man or child with wings. In Sade the ever-present signal of eros is the body part that rises as though it had wings—the soaring prick. If the phallus responds, eros has been summoned for the project of world-making. The following laconic statement from *120 Days of Sodom* lets us know that confession is an activity proper to the Sadeian world: "He goes to confession for the sole purpose of making his confessor's prick rise aloft."

If confession did not belong to the libertine's world, the prick would not soar. Eros defines what is and what is not proper. Founded, therefore, on the erotic impulse, Sade's fiction is an erotic cosmology of the soul. Psychologically, one's desire to confess—to be humbled in the process and to submit to one's confessor—satisfies the soul which signals its pleasure by flapping its phallic wings.

Eros moves in many different directions, so that the worlds of fantasy generated each has its own erotic delights. The eros of one may seem perverted and perverting to the other. Several years ago two psychologists who had been in contact by letter attended a professional conference and met each other for the first time. From the first moment, it was clear to them that there was scant basis for a friendship. The one was quiet, reserved, and somewhat fastidious. The other was loud, lewd, and cantankerous. On the night of their meeting, the quiet one dreamed that he was lying in a bathtub half-filled with water. His new acquaintance came to him, naked, and lay on top of him in the water. The heterosexual dreamer felt pleasure in the contact, but he awoke from the dream feeling quite disturbed.

An erotic movement foreign to familiar waking life had stirred in the dream. In spite of the dreamer's revulsion, the erotic spirit was "mingling" him with something unfamiliar and rejected and yet at the same time pleasurable. The dreamer was being perverted, turned around and through, connected to something alien. The two men were joined face to face in the waters of dissolution, baptism, and transformation. They were like the couple in the illustrations from the "Rosarium Philosophorum" which Jung used in his book on transference. In fact, as an epigraph for this book Jung used a passage that Sade might have appreciated. It is from the alchemist John Gower's book *The Confession of a Lover*: "A warring peace, a sweet wound, a mild evil."

The sweet wound of love can bring us face to face with the persona of another universe, one that feels utterly evil. Sade is not unlike the dream lover who asks us to let him lie erotically on us in the chaotic waters in which our values dissolve. In the dream the form love took was as unacceptable and disturbing as the character of the other person. Romanticized notions of androgyny and the hermaphrodite enjoy the glow of wholeness and resolution of tension. But this Sadeian dream gave the dreamer a powerful but difficult image of union—the homosexual embrace. Sade is a specialist in perverted paths toward psychological cohesion and connection.

Still another ancient source helps put Sade in perspective. The celebrated story told by the second-century Latin writer Apuleius, "Eros and Psyche," contains several Sadeian themes. The story tells how Venus sent her son, Eros, to earth to punish the young Psyche. Psyche fell in love with Eros but then became separated from him. Her movement toward reunion involved four difficult and cruel tasks. During the time of her ordeals, Psyche felt the torture and the onus of loss and impossible effort. Weighed down by so much affliction, she entertained thoughts of suicide. Goddesses usually benevolent cruelly neglected her. Only the wild Pan, whose usual mission is to bring lust and panic to the soul, helped her. Stirred by the primitive presence of Pan, she got on with her tasks, submitting to the hellish nightmare of her condition. Psyche is much like Sade's Justine, looking for love but finding only cruel demands.

When Psyche descended to the lowest pit of hell, pilfering a measure of Persephone's beauty, she was reunited with Eros. One wonders if that phial of Persephone's beauty cream is not the treasure Sade found, as though congenital, in the depths of his own heart. Sade's writing represents that moment in the soul's initiation when it captures the secret of an underworld aesthetic. Persephone is sometimes pictured in monstrous form, with fangs and gorgon-like eyes, not unlike Kali of India. But this, in the underworld, is beauty. Psyche is initiated into the Sadeian aesthetics where ugliness is beauty and where whips, chains, black leather, stiletto heels, brass studs, and technologies of torture have definite appeal. The soul truly finds pleasure in these objects which serve the warrior.

The Apuleius tale implies that torture and pain have roles to play in the maturing of the psyche and in preparing the soul for love. Psyche in a state of pristine innocence cannot sustain a relationship to love. Encouraged by her sisters, that is, by various fantasies sister to innocence, she brings a candle and a knife to the dark, vulnerable bed of Eros. In spite of her innocence, the girlish Psyche can wield a weapon. She can also bring disturbing light to what requires darkness. We will take a close look at Sade's dark and concealed settings, which are foreign to Psyche's upperworld, secular beauty. But after she has submitted to ordeals and has discovered and put on the beauty of Hell, Psyche wins back her attractiveness to Eros. The Sadeian imagination involves an appreciation for the *aesthetics* of perversion, enjoying the delightful horrors it finds in Persephone's boudoir.

James Hillman's study of eros in *The Myth of Analysis* makes two points that apply directly to Sade. First, eros always leads to soul. "Eros is the God of psychic reality," he writes, "the true lord of the psyche, . . . the creative principle which engenders soul and is the patron of the field of psychology."[6] Foolheartedly following his given erotic inclinations, Sade charts a path to soul, indeed a way of recovering soul in a culture that has largely neglected it. Sade's pursuit of eros to the very limits led him into a geography of soul usually left unarticulated and despised.

In this sense, a case might be made for Sade as archetypal psychologist. He tracked eros as revealed to him in his own curiosities and inclinations and surrounded it with an "excess of fantasy," elaborating countless images, experimenting with language and number, keeping close watch on his dreams and letting them guide his imagination. Living for years in dark, uncomfortable, isolated prison cells, he wrote plays, essays, novels, stories, and letters, all of which poke at the limits of the polite world-view. Sade is often called a forerunner—of Freud or Krafft-Ebing or Nietzsche—and maybe he is a precursor for imaginal psychology as well. Like Keats, he shows how soul-making is carried out by transforming the stuff of everyday life into carefully articulated imagery whose style is determined by one's daimon and by the vicissitudes of life.

Hillman's second point is that the soul is typically tortured by eros in an initiatory movement. "For whatever the disguise, what is taking place is the creative eros connecting with an awakening psyche. All the turns and torments are part of—shall we say Bhakti yoga?—a psychological discipline of eros development, or an erotic discipline of psychological development, aiming toward psychic integration and erotic identity."[7]

In the Apuleius story, Psyche gets a taste of love and then suffers his absence. But during that separation she goes through an extraordinary initiation. What she feels as loss is actually gain. The impossible demands made upon her are not anti-erotic. In the end they are revealed to have been in the service of eros all along. It was similar for Sade himself. He tasted a few of the delights of dark eros in the flesh, but then he was put in prison for years where those experiences blossomed into a more psychological experience and expression. Sardonically he tells his jailers that if they were smart they would have locked him up with prostitutes until he had "used up all the oil in his lamp." Then he would have been tamed. But forced abstinence had a different result. "You have made a mistake, you have heated my head, you have made me conjure up phantoms which I shall now have to realize. . . . If you overboil the stew, you know, it may well boil over."[8]

In Sade eros boiled over into writing. His biography demonstrates that perverted desires claiming so much of a life can actually be the foundation for soul-making, "an erotic discipline of psychological development." We might think of Sade's taunts when we have to deal with compulsive abuse, victimization, people exposing themselves, sado-masochistic practices, incest, and other "perversions"—turnings—of eros. Oddly, Sade may point to an appropriate therapy, a way of bringing imagination to these difficult twists of erotic desire. They may need containment (prison), where they can transform into poetic expression. Very concretely, we may learn from Sade to write letters from this place, to find an aesthetic in it—a style and a special language. Therapy of perverting eros is not getting rid of it, but allowing it to find its subtle body, a sublimation from complex to articulated fantasy.

Sade teaches us, too, that our naive expectations to change the direction of eros are entirely misguided. In 1783 he wrote: "Imperious, choleric, impetuous, extreme in everything, of a disorderly wealth of imagination on human conduct such as life never saw the equal of, there you have me in a couple of words; one thing more, you must either kill me or take me as I am, for I shall not change."[9] Whatever it is that inspires the love of images oblique to norms and standards should not be killed off or wished away. It can be placed in a secure container where its images will boil up into articulate forms. This is the essence of soul-making. Sade's suffering drove him toward literature. Our suffering can force us into image. Tormenting Eros eventually marries with Psyche.

Various paths of imagination differ in quality and accent. The Sadeian imagination is remarkably dark and erotic. While characters in fiction may be primarily in the heroic mode or on a salvational quest or on a search for meaning, Sade's characters are tracking down their erotic needs, sensitive to signs of erotic satisfaction and displeasure. The Sadeian imagination, then, in a larger sense, has this erotic emphasis. What world has to be made, it asks, for eros to be evoked?

The Sadeian libertine answers that question by exploring the most revolting necessities of the soul. All those things which we try to avoid or conquer in our sentimentality or our puritanism or our enthronement of the good and pure, those things the Sadeian figure looks to with promise and hope. In order to explore the Sadeian imagination, we are required to suspend moral belief and entertain notions that border on the absurd. Is there any value hidden in the core of abuse, violence, perversion, and incest? Do the odd sexual couplings and scatological extravagances of our dreams instruct us positively in the nature of the psyche? Does love of the perverted have a place in the opus of the soul?

The erotic pull in the Sadeian imagination leads to unsettling possibilities. We can read Apuleius and develop an inspiring psychology of development, but when we find Sade picturing the mansion of Persephone as a place full of guile and putrefaction, then the initiation of psyche demands a darkening of values. The last ordeal is the ultimate surrender of upperworld norms. Sade, devoted to the fourth degree of psyche's initiation, casts a deep blue light on everything in sight. He forces us to feel the textures of the shadow and to smell the foul things with which the soul is mysteriously in love. Moreover, he does it all with perverted joy and distorted beauty.

3.

The Ravishing of Innocence

An uglifier needs raw material for his work, something of considerable splendor and beauty to violate, a Mona Lisa on which to draw a moustache. Sade didn't have to look far for a suitable object for satire and attack. His chief target was Christianity and the morality of the "pale Galilean," to use a phrase from one of his admirers, Swinburne. But more generally his concern was innocence itself, a virtue he exposes as a vice and embodies in one of the most pathetic characters in his fiction, Justine.

Critics complain that Sade fails to develop his characters, giving us skeletal types rather than full figures. But in the case of the archetypal innocent, Justine, simplicity is a primary attribute. Justine personifies girlish innocence. Uncomplicated, naive, and obvious, she is like simple Psyche in the Apuleius story, like Alice naively exposed to the more worldly Gryphon. This is how Sade describes her in the novel:

> A virginal air, large blue eyes very soulful and appealing, a dazzling fair skin, a supple and resilient body, a touching voice, teeth of ivory and the loveliest blond hair, there you have a sketch of this charming creature whose naive graces and delicate traits are beyond our power to describe. (459)

A Hollywood picture of virginal charm, blue-eyed and blond, this image says something about innocence itself. It is a young girl, puella, attractive and charming, the embodiment of moral and religious ideals. You see her walking out of churches on a Sunday morning, crisp and clean. She sits in every classroom, free of guile and not the type, she says in her demeanor and appearance, to be irresponsible. She appears in people, men and women, sometimes as true innocence, sometimes as a conceit. She can be a true virgin or a beguiling coquette.

One sees the mask of Justine worn by people who use innocence to avoid the harsh realities that life presents or that well up from the heart. *In-nocere* in Latin can mean either not to hurt or not to be hurt. Both are present in the Justine pattern, that compelling need to see oneself and to be seen as beyond reproach. The Justine innocent may not have felt the stings of life and therefore lives a partial consciousness, a girlish simplicity. Or, she is not capable of aggression and will not intentionally hurt anyone under any circumstances. Such sensitive people cannot edit a manuscript or correct a student's paper or honestly advise a friend, precisely because they cannot be the agent of hurt, even with the best of motives.

Justine is not only a type of person or a figure active in a personality; she is also a social syndrome. Sade inveighed against this puella he saw all around him in his chaotic society. Indeed, he was the victim of this style that parades its purity but is potentially violent and dangerous. When a state proclaims the innocence of its motives and methods, Justine speaks. When a modern government says publicly that its primary goal is peace, and yet that government puts most of its money into weaponry that would make Sade's technologies look harmless,

Justine is constellated. It may not be clear on the surface whether this girlhood is pure posturing or if she is deeply embedded in the personality of a nation. Justine symptoms hint at a loss of the puella of the soul, displaying in ineffective and exaggerated form attitudes that could be valuable and useful if they were more grounded and authentic. Justine innocence on a national level might indicate a desperate need for genuine innocence and the dewy vitality of psychological girlhood.

In his essay on the "bad mother," James Hillman emphasizes the tandem structure in archetypal patterns.[1] Since usually one figure implies or constellates another, to talk of the archetypal mother may imply an archetypal child. Often we are tempted into an oppositional interpretation of this tandem, forcing a choice of one side over the other. But Hillman recommends an attitude that embraces the tandem with its tensions and ambiguities. This observation applies in the case of Justine, the archetypal innocent.

Sade places Justine within the context of the cruel, usually male, libertine whose lust in the face of sweet innocence leads to violence. The erotic response of the libertine is heightened by the presence of this charming, naive girl, as the following passage from *Justine* reveals. Justine is describing her treatment at the hands of two cruel men:

> . . . their language is of the most violent, the sentence pronounced upon me appalling: it is nothing less than a question of a vivisection in order to inspect the beating of my heart, and upon this organ to make observations which cannot practicably be made upon a cadaver. Meanwhile, I am undressed, and subjected to the most impudicious fondlings.
>
> "Before all else," says Rombeau, "my opinion is a stout

> attack ought to be delivered upon the fortress your lenient proceedings have respected. . . . Why, 'tis superb! do you mark that velvet texture, the whiteness of those two half-moons defending the portal! never was there a virgin of such freshness." (555–56)

The virgin and the dirty old man go together as a tandem. One elicits the other. The natural tendency, of course, is to side with the innocent girl and feel revulsion toward the libertine. But Sade takes the opposite stance. If the reader can suspend his "natural" belief in the girl and give Sade a sympathetic hearing, then the tensions of this tandem are restored. The Sadeian viewpoint liminally embraces both innocence and corruption.

Innocence and Inspection

In the passage quoted, Justine elicits the curiosity of the libertine who then engages in one of his characteristic acts: inspection. Innocence inspires inspection. What kind of heart could be so innocent? the libertine inquires. He must inspect it in its living state so as to understand it. Obviously, the horror of literally inspecting a living heart is part of the Sadeian tone. But that tone carries over into the image. Inspection itself, of any kind, partakes of the libertine's cruelty. Every examination of the soul involves Sadeian vivisection.

Science has investigated every inch of innocent nature, and often the inspection has been accomplished *in vivo*. Not only is the physical world subject to all kinds of instruments and measures and dissections, psychologically and sociologically the soul has been put under a microscope. An old joke tells that the family tree of a Pacific Island people includes father, mother, children, uncles, aunts, and anthropologist. Science performs these vivisections innocently.

It is not insignificant that people who submit, masochistically, to scientific experiment are called *sub-jects*, a word which means "pressed under" and is used of citizens in a monarchy. The world and its people are the innocent *subjects* of scientific inspection. This is not to say, siding sentimentally with Justine, that there is anything wrong in itself with scientific curiosity and inspection. But the passage does lead us to ponder the Sadeian nature of what usually appears to be "pure" science.

Recognizing the Sadeian theme in all kinds of inspection, whether or not coupled with vivisection, serves several psychological purposes. For example, it allows us to glimpse the "who's" in the action. A scientific experimenter in the field may look not only innocent but positively benign and caring as he totes his instruments for the study of animals and habitats. But if he is inspecting innocent nature, he may, especially from its point of view, have a more pernicious attitude and occupation. The fact that some notorious psychological studies have resulted in extreme sadistic behavior suggests a Sadeian element in all such studies, a less than innocent intent that occasionally breaks through to consciousness.

Sade's imagery of inspection also alerts us to the fact that, even though it may go unnoticed, there is suffering involved. Nature suffers from our inspection of it, even though we tend to think of nature as inert and therefore beyond suffering. Chemical companies making our fruit look fresher, our lawns greener, and our sugary treats tastier are preying upon innocence when it turns out they have been giving us tumors. We have granted science and its applications carte blanche and presumption of innocence. Justine believes that her tormentors have her best interests at heart. If business could sustain the ambiguity of its efforts—helping in one way, killing in another—we might find a way to deal with nature aggressively without complete loss of actual innocence. We also might end the killing and torturing that can only be sustained by the denial of libertinage in business and technology.

Sade's imagery also brings to light certain literalisms and acting-out. Harmless, if pain-giving, inspection easily turns into sadistic torture. Deny or repress the Sadeian character of investigation and study, and these obviously benign activities take on a dark character. Nuclear scientists working on the atomic bomb in its early stages apparently came late to the realization that the marquis had a hand in their work.

This characteristic delight of the libertine, inspecting what is virginal, may seem so natural and ordinary in the modern world that we take it for granted and are unaware of the pain our efforts bring to Earth, to society, and to individuals. When the pattern is split we lose, too, our own virginal innocence. The problem in bulldozing a tree is not merely its loss. The psychological danger is loss of virginal feeling. Justine's despair is also the soul speaking. In the Sadeian activity of clearing land belong feelings for both the needs of culture and the ruin of the innocent tree. The tandem includes both sides. Ecological issues are always psychological, as they are filled with fantasy. When two sides meet to argue the needs of civilization versus the ruin of nature, a Sadeian dialogue is re-enacted: the spoilers against the sentimentalists. But these polarized discussions will continue as long as the underlying issue—the denial of innocence or the denial of Sadeian aggression—is not resolved.

Exposing oneself to inspection is a masochistic act. The libertines look closely at the most intimate parts of the body. From the perspective of the examined one, usually a woman, her most private being is laid open to the judgmental eyes of her tormentors. The Sadeian pattern, always both masochistic and sadistic in tone, includes exposing oneself. Human life requires a degree of openness (masochism) and a degree of aggressive inspecting (sadism). When this tandem breaks apart, it takes symptomatic forms: people too willing to present themselves to science for study, for example, and researchers too willing to subject people to analysis. If a person goes to a physician masochistically, he constellates the sadist in the doctor; but if there is no submission at all, there can be no effective inspection. The doctor cannot see what is not exposed.

Both inspecting and being inspected have a place. Monastic life wove into the day's activities a practice called "examination of conscience," an internal exposure of oneself to oneself, an inspection for the purpose of soul-work. Spiritual guidance, counseling, analysis, therapy, education—they all engage in this Sadeian practice of close, minute, personal, intimate revelation and examination. The innocent "victim" of inspection resists, as psychoanalysis says, this inspection, but resistance could be imagined, with Sade in mind, as an archetypal move, Justine's proper inhibition. Resistance to inspection is part of the pattern and is not necessarily an ego defense. We resist exposure, but then we are overcome by the libertine (liberating) desire to see at close hand. Again, as is so often the case in Sade, the *felix culpa*, the fortunate failure to resist fully and the overcoming of innocent self-protection, allows insight. *Insight*, a word used so often in psychology, is Sadeian, the work of the libertine on a willing subject.

The Deepening of Innocence

The Justine–libertine tandem holds together tightly. Justine's innocence inflames the libertines. The more she exposes her naivete, the more they want her. They have a cultivated taste for her innocence and suffering. The following is another scene from the novel:

> And the cruel men, having laid hands upon me, dragged me toward the wood, laughing at my tears and screams.
>
> "We'll tie each of her members to a tree—we need four trees placed in a rectangle," said Bressac, tearing off my clothes.
>
> Then by means of their cravats, their handkerchiefs, their braces, they make cords wherewith I am tied instantly, in keeping with their plan, that is to say in the cruelest and most painful position imaginable. I cannot express to you what I suffered; it seemed they were rending me limb from limb and that my belly facing downward and strained to the utmost, was about to split at any moment, sweat drenched my forehead, I no longer existed save through the violence of pain; had it ceased to compress my nerves, a mortal anguish would surely have seized me: the villains were amused by my posture, they considered me and applauded. (507)

They considered and applauded. These cruel men love to see the innocent girl naked, stretched, full of pain, humiliated. Notice what the libertine does to innocence: he exposes it, stretches it out, humiliates it.

Innocence in fact calls for these Sadeian reactions because it tends to be haughty. The libertines bring it down, "belly downward," and stretch it out carefully for inspection. This rough treatment happens in psychotherapy all the time: the therapist notices the innocence of a patient, exposes it, inspects it, probes it, and in a sense applauds the uncomfortable feelings that accompany the analysis. The therapy must be going somewhere, he thinks: the patient is getting uncomfortable.

C. G. Jung was concerned in much of his writing with this issue of innocence. For him, innocence generates a shadow, a dark, unconscious, potentially evil figure who is an inversion of the genteel persona presented to the world. This shadow is often projected, cast out into the world so that convenient individuals can serve as scapegoats. In Jung's words:

> The individual loses his guilt and exchanges it for infantile innocence; once more he can blame the wicked father for this and the unloving mother for that, and all the time he is caught in this inescapable causal nexus like a fly in a spider's web, without noticing that he has lost his moral freedom. But no matter how much parents and grandparents may have sinned against the child, the man who is really adult will accept these sins as his own condition which has to be reckoned with. Only a fool is interested in other people's guilt, since he cannot alter it. The wise man learns only from his own guilt. He will ask himself: Who am I that all this should happen to me? To find the answer to this fateful question he will look into his own heart.[2]

Tempted to take sides in this Sadeian tandem of innocence and cruelty, we would rather identify with Justine and project the libertine. In that act we get rid of guilt and bask in innocence. Then the innocent one only "feels guilty," which is different from appropriating one's actual guilt. "The wise man," Jung says, "learns only from his own guilt." He looks into his own heart, a phrase that echoes Sade's intentions as a novelist—to ask why this should happen to me. This is not exactly loss of innocence; it is more finding the tandem to innocence. Feelings of guilt invite us to complete innocence with a look at our own cruelty. As a symptom, feeling guilty sustains innocence, but it also invites responsibility. Following through on feelings of guilt might eventually lead to an effective realization of guilt.

Both Justine and the libertine, both innocence and cruelty, are elements in the Sadeian pattern. As Hillman says, two poles "are as they are because they are locked together in a tandem which affects the nature of each."[3] When such a pattern is not split into a schizoid polarity, one side influences and has an impact upon the other. In a tight configuration, innocence is ever exposed, examined, and penetrated—initiated—and the aggressive, spoiling, processing capacities are also tempered and qualified by purity of heart. Aggression remains in touch with sensitivity; innocence abandons its hubris.

Jung's suggestion—to look at the innocence and guilt in our own hearts—is a challenge because such a shift in perspective, away from innocence, is painful. Jung is advising us, in effect, to play the libertine on ourselves. Our eyes become the instruments of a torturing examination. The moment we cease identifying with the innocent puella, we lose a certain basis for self-worth. Like Justine, we lie exposed. But the other side applauds, enjoying this necessary corruption of purity. In fact, actual joy erupts when this shadow is let out of the prison of repression. The pleasure Sade's libertines enjoy in their wicked rituals reflects the joy anyone might feel when the dark tandem to innocence is released into life.

To "own" the libertine, and not just girlishness, implies that one can transcend the boundaries of a morality and propriety that give the ego a certain effective, yet narrow, supporting structure. Being innocent, we can feel fine about ourselves. The Sadeian point, however, is to find self-acceptance even in the presence of genuine guilt. Imagine a government that acknowledged its capacity for violence, that offered no pretense to false innocence. It could be strong without loss of true innocence. If the United States were to examine its soul in light of Hiroshima, it would not lose innocence altogether, but it might be initiated into a new attitude where honesty of intention and genuine power might coexist.

The Sadeian perspective is clearly more cold-hearted than our usual warm and fuzzy posture. One of Justine's tormentors goes by the name Coeur-de-fer, Heart of Iron. Iron, the metal of Mars, is central to the alchemy of Sade, who gives metallic Mars a place in the planetary round of the soul. He understands that it takes a hardening of the heart to acknowledge reasons for guilt deeply enough. A Sadeian appreciation for iron in the alchemy of the soul encourages firmness and a lasting structure.

Sade not only gives iron-heartedness a place of honor, he also inverts the principle that virtue has its own rewards. Time after time his despicable libertines receive extravagant praise and tangible reward. Roland, for instance, who tortured Justine and then hanged her for a while and nailed her in a coffin—various ways one might try to deal with innocence—has good luck with his material fortunes:

> He received the immense quantity of Venetian funds he had wished. . . . the scoundrel could not possibly have enjoyed

> better luck, he was going to leave with an income of two million, not to mention his hopes of getting more; this was the new piece of evidence Providence had prepared for me. This was the latest manner in which it wished to convince me that prosperity belongs to Crime only and indigence to virtue. (*Justine*, 686)

In the Sadeian world, crime not only pays, it pays well. Psychologically, suspending one's innocence and nailing down one's purity can have its true and perhaps unexpected rewards. But frothy fantasies of reward often accompany innocence. The pure of heart think they deserve pie in the sky, unending bliss after death, or even mundane success. Sade corrects that naive expectation, reminding us that the other side has its own pleasures and honors. Sade's remarks about surprise rewards for the vicious contradict a deep belief that innocence will always be rewarded and evil punished. Justine's sudden discovery that evil has its benefits comes as a shock to her, as it would to anyone identified with innocence. Justine is forever being confronted with Job's problem: why does innocence suffer and evil prosper?

Highest among the institutions that embody the split between innocence and cruelty is religion. Religion stands for innocence. Therefore, it is not surprising that along her path Justine should present her purity to the church:

> We enter the church; the doors are closed; a lamp is lit near the confessional. Dom Severino bids me assume my place, he sits down and requests me to tell him everything with complete confidence.
>
> I was perfectly at ease with a man who seemed so mild-mannered, so full of gentle sympathy. I disguised nothing

> from him: I confessed all my sins; I related all my miseries; I even uncovered the shameful mark wherewith the barbaric Rodin had branded me. Severino listened to everything with keenest attention, he even had me repeat several details, wearing always a look of pity and of interest. (*Justine*, 562)

Sweet, young, devout Justine—her name tells her nature—has just undergone untold misery and now arrives at a monastery, St. Mary-of-the-Wood, to find some comfort. She should have known that this was no ordinary monastery, and she might have guessed from the name of the prior, Severino, the severe one, that her trust would not be well placed with him and his monks. But innocence is blind to the clues of its own corruption. It fails to see the instruments of initiation within its own revered structures, in this case religion.

In Justine Sade reveals the absurd tenacity of innocence, its habit to maintain itself in face of the most blatant contradictions. Innocence is held by an inertia that can be stupid and blind. It does not want to be corrupted, and it will insist for as long as possible that evil is not real.

In practice, of course, religion is extremely Sadeian, forcing beliefs upon its devotees "under pain of eternal damnation," to use words one actually finds in religious teaching. Churchgoers submit to all kinds of pain, self-denial, and subjugation for a worthy cause. Again, to note these dynamics and to recognize their Sadeian slant is not to say they are inherently negative. But maybe we should know that the entire Sadeian system infuses itself into such a pure institution as the church. Attention to the high aspirations of spirituality can camouflage its Sadeian strains. Indeed, Dom Severino's behavior in the confessional is not entirely foreign to actual priests and counselors.

Is there not something Sadeian in the voyeuristic practices of spiritual guidance, counseling, and analysis? And, is not the Sadeian element in these highly regarded activities generally concealed and denied, made subject to all the unfortunate distortions of repression? People looking for a counselor or spiritual guide might be wise to choose someone who knows the Sadeian nature of the profession.

In recent times we have seen many extreme examples of the sado-masochistic potential of religion: Jim Jones leading his followers to mass suicide and several gurus and their followers turning to violence and sexual anarchy. Spiritual and psychological leaders in the human potential movement, working at centers of renewal, profess sincere ideals and yet act out their cruel shadows. Mainstream churches demonstrate their own more covert tendencies toward authoritarianism and hellfire-and-brimstone emotional terrorizing. Any institution professing high and innocent ideals exposes itself to the dangers of radical sado-masochistic polarizing.

Another connection between St. Mary-of-the-Wood and Sade is the point Roland Barthes makes: there is an extraordinary parallel between what goes on in monastic life, or spiritual practice, and in Sadeian ritual. Whenever the spirit becomes activated—whether a woman runs off to a convent or to India, or a man takes up a strict regimen of physical fitness—the soul may feel battered by the spirit's demands. When we say a person "makes a religion" out of exercise or work, that is not a light metaphor. All attempts to give strict form to life, even if they are based in a fantasy of self-improvement, participate in Sadeian monastic ideals.

Rites of Initiation

Returning to the principle that Sade need not be taken as an anomaly, a man with a problem, but rather as a mythographer in his own right, we might note some correspondences between the painful rites depicted so precisely in his fiction and similar imagery in religion. For instance, we can make a quick shift from innocence to innocents. In the liturgical year of Christendom, the festival of the Holy Innocents—the children killed by Herod at the time of Jesus' birth—was long a popular feast. Curiously, it was celebrated in ways that would charm the heart of the Divine Marquis.

In France, Childermas, the feast of the children, was known as the Festival of Fools (*Fête des Fous*). At the beginning of the carnival period, deacons elected a Pope of Fools, a Bishop of Innocents, and an Abbot of Ninnies. These exalted figures presided over orgies, dances, games, profane songs, and parodies of the holy liturgy. Priests wore masks, dressed as women, and sang obscene chants. The altar was made into a tavern, the scene of dice and card games. A smelly old shoe was burned in place of incense. At Beauvais a young girl rode on the back of an ass, imitating the story of the Flight into Egypt.

In some places on Childermas, a boy was made bishop, and priests wore their vestments inside out and held their books upside down. These "perversions" took place in such well-known churches as St. Paul's of London and All Souls' at Oxford.

Justine's sister Juliette, who aspired to the rank of libertine, celebrated with the pope a Satanic mass that closely resembles the rites of Childermas. After the pope has desecrated St. Peter's altar with Juliette, she exclaims: "Sodomized by the Pope, the body of Jesus Christ nestled in one's ass, oh, my friends! what rare delight." (*Juliette*, 802)

Childermas had other Sadeian themes. In some places young boys cut green plants and boughs from trees and whipped the girls. The practice, according to Frazer, was called "whipping with fresh green." When the boys whipped the girls, they recited ritual words indicating that the girls should consider the whipping a blessing and that the boys should be rewarded. This is all very Sadeian. Of course, one could take it literally and immediately be offended at the sexism in the practice. But from another point of view entirely, it is the puella who is being initiated in this festival of innocence.

There was also an element of carnival license in Childermas, a transcendence of the perimeters of morality. As carnival, it included a joyful erotic acknowledgment of evil. The inversion of custom and sanctity occasioned joy. New pleasures were to be found in the exploration of things usually considered evil. In particular, pious leaders transformed into clowns, so that authority itself turned inside out, to the great relief of those suffering the burden of ecclesiastical domination.

In life, authority and law can be difficult to bear, especially if you are the subject. Sade reveals the pleasures of exercising authority. In his sexual rituals, authority is abstracted from the usual social environment and revealed as an enjoyable thing in itself. Some of its pleasure comes from its very heaviness, as an antidote to the lightness of innocence and victimization. Authoritarian figures are presented as erotic: bishops, jailkeepers, hangmen, lords, the pope. These figures in life and in the psyche offer deep pleasures that may be denied as we typically identify with victims and subjects. Psychologically, the soul can suffer from the repression of these figures, although it may take a strong Sadeian stomach to give them a place.

The libertine penetrates innocence, opens it up, finds its blood. In this, too, Sade echoes rites of passage. In the temperate rites of modern religion, the bishop approaches a young person to be confirmed and slaps him on the face gently. But Mircea Eliade and others report sacred initiatory scenes in which young people in rites of maturity suffer terrible physical pain and emotional terror at the hands of their benevolent families. Eliade gives the following example from the Karadjeri people of Australia:

> . . . about the age of twelve, the boy is taken into the bush, and there he is anointed from head to foot with human blood. Some few months later his nose is pierced and a quill is introduced into the wound; the boy then receives a special name. The second and most important rite, that of circumcision, takes place two or three years later. . . . The boy then remains on the ground, with a shield over his knees; and the men come to him one by one, and let the blood flowing from their opened veins drip down upon his head.[4]

These are mysterious rites that cannot be explained simply by saying that pain toughens and matures a young person or even that images of blood and wounding symbolize death to childhood. The blood, the opening of the skin, the wounding of the penis—all of these powerful images transform the young man. He is not the same as he was before this experience. He has experienced pain in a religious, ritual setting, where its mystery is given priority. Cruel initiation is a way toward a deeper sensibility.

In our own world, too, obviously more secular than the community Eliade describes, pain, blood, and sexual wounding signal an initiatory process. Wounding and attack initiate the innocent into a deeper sense of life, less removed from suffering and aggression. The Karadjeri elders are not evil people, but they are not innocent. They are neither bad guys nor good guys, and in that tension of innocence and guilt lies a truth Justine-like innocents learn through painful initiation.

Sade's fictional orgies, highly ritualized in form, can be seen as initiations, deepening innocence through pain. The libertines correspond to the Karadjeri elders who torture and frighten their young charges out of a childish world-view and sensibility. The Sadeian vision, then, does not entail one-sided violence, as the clinical term *sadism* would suggest, but rather a pattern of innocence and guilt, two postures drawn to each other. Justine keeps running into Severinos, Bressacs, Rolands, and Hearts-of-Iron. The libertines seek out comely virgins as the perfect answer to their erotic cravings. Libertines and virgins need each other because each is incomplete in itself. They are opposite ends of a polarity that is destructive, not because of the quality of its components, but because of the distance between them.

Psychology recognizes that an individual's narcissism can be wounded and that this wounding is all for the good. Self-absorbed individuals content with their own solipsistic philosophies sometimes feel "wounded" when some event fortunately punctures their carefully nurtured ways. In a similar way we could speak of a "Justine wound," the puncturing of innocence in which feelings of loss and pain stab the heart. Yet those pains ripen the soul, acquaint it more intimately with the ways of nature, and carry it beyond the simplistic ideals of youth.

Everyone has his or her own master of the dungeon who inflicts his special kind of pain: loneliness, unrequited love, jealousy, envy, grief. We speak easily of self-torture, but dreams make it clear, as do the hallucinations of psychotic people, that the inner figure who tortures has a face or several faces. If we knew the "persons" behind those faces, we might understand the telos of torture and the necessity of the Sadeian libertine who haunts the psyche. Often we overlook the libertine within because we assume that the torment is coming from the world, from another person, from some past trauma, or from some social ill. But this is nothing more than sophisticated scapegoating. If a person is suffering, then there is someone turning the screws, someone whose job it is to tend the chamber of horrors.

The other side of the tandem—the innocent one—is equally difficult to imagine. Although we identify easily with being victimized and hurt, this identification is not the same as entertaining the figure of the puella. If the libertine is one of the great repressed figures of our time, then so, too, is the wide-eyed girl. Justine seems so naive, time after time walking into the opportunities of her corruption. This, too, is a Sadeian image. Rather than trying always to leave innocence, to grow up out of it, to smarten it up, to finally learn never to be a victim, the Sadeian approach suggests that we embrace our innocence, entering it fully without all the qualifications. Allowing Justine a place among the figures of the psyche is a move toward reconciliation with the libertine. Paradoxically, to become more profoundly naive is to discover power, aggression, and assertiveness.

Sade presents us with tableaux of our torments, giving face, voice, and personality to the source of our suffering. Sadism is an abstract idea, but Sadeian fiction is a wealth of imagery, a theater of torture that provides the scenery and casts the drama in which innocence presents its naivete and then is inspected, opened, bled, and penetrated.

4.

Fundaments and Excrements

> Let us suppose, for example, that this desire were to see a particular part of your body and that, through clumsiness, you were to exhibit some other—you appreciate to what extent such contempt would be upsetting to our imaginations, and you are aware of all that one risks by chilling the mind of a libertine who, let us presume, is expecting a behind for his pleasure, and to whom some fool presents the mons veneris. By and large, offer your fronts very little to our sight; remember that this loathesome part, which only the alienation of her wits could have permitted Nature to create, is always the one we find most repugnant. (*120 Days of Sodom*, 252)

This passage is from the long, plotless laundry-list of debauchery Sade wrote in prison on a long, narrow band of paper. The Duc is addressing women who are about to serve their masters, reminding them that it is their duty to interpret the desires of their lords.

Once again Sade turns the world upside down. For him the body has its peculiar organization and hierarchies. The mons veneris, Venus's bower, is at the bottom of his list of erotic priorities, and the "bottom" is at the top. While Freud's body is focused on three parts—mouth, anus, and penis—and the Tantric body has seven focal centers, and certain puritan bodies have fig leaves for genitals, the Sadeian body faces backward, with the bottom in full view.

Venus upsets the imaginations of the libertines. Although occasionally Sade refers to Venusian pleasures in a general way and includes libertine delights among them, ordinarily the libertine is not interested in Venus: she chills his mind. The union of male and female in loving embrace; the enjoyment of the female form and what makes it female; gauzy, romantic sensuality—these are not part of the Sadeian life. Even Sade's writing style lacks Venusian qualities. In spite of all its raw sexuality, it isn't pornographic in the usual sense. The situations he presents are scandalous and lascivious, but they are not depicted in sensuous detail. The mechanics of the debauchery are more important than the textures.

In the Sadeian universe the presiding deity is not Venus. We have to look for another archetypal focus, a different God to rule the realm of the libertine. Hints as to who this God might be include qualities peculiar to the libertine style: anality, ritualized orgies, emphasis on number and counting, rigid hierarchies, distant relationships, a plethora of abstract theories, strict rules, and a negative yet constant attention to religion. All of these qualities point to a single deity from the Western tradition: Saturn.

It was customary in literature of the Middle Ages and Renaissance, as well as in painting and poetry, to ascribe each part of life to a classical deity. Sometimes this practice took the specific form of astrology. Many astrological paintings and murals were intended as reminders of the Gods within ordinary life.[1] But usually the God or Goddess was simply known to "rule" over a particular sphere of life, and those whose occupations and personal traits fitted within the sphere of that God were called his children. To know the God presiding over an activity was to know something about the deepest roots of that activity, about its most profound context and origins.

If Sade's fictional universe is indeed Saturnine, then we might expect it to differ altogether from the Venusian, although surface details may seem to confuse the two. We might also expect the Sadeian world to operate on principles at odds with standard values, since Saturn's style was never understood to be particularly benign and graceful.

In the tradition deriving from Greek and Roman religion, Saturn was known as the distant, cold, philosophical, theological, mystical, dry, and quiet God, as well as the archon of melancholy and artistic genius.[2] Among his "children" were geometers, carpenters, latrine cleaners, and grave diggers. Death, abstraction, filth, construction—all of these were within the domain of Saturn. And, since Saturn was identified with the Greek God Chronos, he was also the patron of the Golden Age, the Old Father who felt threatened by his sons and therefore swallowed them and whose father Ouranos's genitals were the raw material forming Aphrodite from the sea. In modern language we might say that the Saturnine embraces abstract thought, fantasies of a golden past, old age, anality, order, depression, deep mystical and artistic reflection, and emotional coldness and distance.

Although it is too easy to say simply that Sade was carrying on the tradition of Saturn, an appreciation for this imagery does provide a context for the strange erotic inclinations and various points of style among Sade's libertines. Sade's deconstruction of religion, for example, emphasizing the corruption of innocence, is clearly Saturnine, given the God's role of taking thoughts to the highest, coldest, most refined theological outposts. Saturn was known to be constricting, binding, and severe—qualities much revered by the Sadeian masters.

Saturn is not easily loved. Old medical texts of the Middle Ages and Renaissance link Saturn with Mars and label them malevolent deities, important to human life but difficult and poisonous. Distance, hard-heartedness, and a lust for cruelty are not attractive, yet when they are more than crass misanthropy, when they filter a subtle shadow into the make-up of a person, they can be seen to have a place in human relations. It may be painfully cruel for a teacher to tell a young admirer that she doesn't want to marry him, but in the long run that infliction of pain is beneficent. Saturn can be bitter medicine, but he is medicine nonetheless.

The God is known not only in the activities of life that imitate his peculiar virtues but also in the body, since it is traditional to ascribe astrological planets to specific body parts. In view of Saturn's notorious act of swallowing his children, the mouth might seem, under certain circumstances, Saturnine. But he is also attached to another, lower area.

We tend to think of the body as a thing, a fact, a given. But the body is always an imagined body. A physician, an anatomist, an artist, and a lover will imagine a particular body differently. Varied meanings and emotions will inform a person's experience of the body depending upon the imagination. Throughout history the body has been treated allegorically: the eye as judgment, the heart as feeling, and the head as intelligence. Astrology assigns the body parts planetary meanings. But the body is also a collection of images less definitely related to specific symbols. A body part can suggest a great world of metaphoric significance.

To Sade's characters the anatomical part of greatest delight and importance is the backside. As well Sade personally confessed to this erotic penchant. In 1775 on a trip to Italy he was deeply stirred by the "divine forms of every limb and the graceful rotundities of bosom and buttocks of the Venus de Medici." He was also enthusiastic about the "voluptuous backside" of a statue of a hermaphrodite. (*Juliette*, 614)

In Sade's metaphoric universe the backside takes on cosmological significance. It is a statement about the soul, an object of eros not simply as a fetish but as a signal of meaning. In Plato the eyes are the windows of the soul; in courtly love the heart is an organ of intense longing; in modern popular thought the brain is the seat of intelligence—in Sade the backside is an intensely erotic presentation.

The Root Metaphor of Gender

In Sade's fiction, attention to the rear, for example, diminishes the relevance of gender. When attention is focused on the buttocks and anus, differences between the genders become less prominent. Sade's orgies take their special form from the fact that men and women are treated equally, so to speak. Juliette, Justine's worldly sister, describes the following scene from her visit to Italy:

> [My two admirers] devour me, but in the Italian style: my backside becomes the unique object of their caresses, they both kiss it, tongue it, nibble it, worry it; they make tireless and prolonged to-do over it, cannot get their fill of it, and behave for all the world as if they are unaware I am a woman. (*Juliette*, 738)

The libertines disregard gender, turn women into men and men into women. They don't want to see the fronts of bodies where gender would be obvious. They like genderlessness, inverting the non-Sadeian slogan *Vive la difference*! Therefore, once again Sade counters the familiar sentimental world-view in which life is a marriage of all that is different and imagined as male and female. Loving and appreciating sameness, Sade has no interest in harmonizing opposites.

Loss of gender is, in fact, a significant element in modern life. This is Ivan Illich's point in his book *Gender*, that modern society has replaced a sense of gender with sex, sexism, and sexuality, all abstractions that treat the person as a commodity. Modern economics, he says, has made us all neuters, with the concomitant loss of body, home, and place. When we lose gender, we lose "vernacular" life, our individuality, our concrete existence. "Gender shapes bodies," he writes, "as they shape space and are in turn shaped by its arrangements."[3] For Illich, gender is crucial in overcoming the depersonalization of the industrial age.

Illich regards the failure to appreciate gender as a symptom of our time. This failure appears in our abstract talk about "sexuality." In Illich's opinion the word should never be used. He implies that such enterprises as sex education and sex therapies, especially those of a biological and mechanical kind, tend to make sex abstract and, by focusing imagination on organs and right postures, dissipate gender sensibility. In effect, these methods accomplish symptomatically what Sade's libertines do in erotic ritual—they delight in sameness.

A Sadeian analysis also looks at an unsexed society, but it suggests that the abstraction of sex is symptomatic of a desire in the soul for a life not based on gender. Whereas Illich is complaining about loss, Sade demonstrates that there is a deep yearning for life without gender. In other words, from a Sadeian point of view our current symptomatic loss of gender paradoxically points to a need for genderlessness. The Saturnine vision disregards pieties about gender love. Instead of seeing the progress of the soul through romanticized images of the feminine, as in courtly love poetry, Sade cold-heartedly imagines the soul's work as anal. Instead of seeing the goal of soul-work as a mating of male and female, as a hierosgamos or sacred marriage, or as a hermaphrodite or yin and yang—images Jung so often cites—Sade presents a genderless ideal. All division and duality are abandoned in favor of the union of like with like. Sade's ideal is not homosexuality as much as uni-sexuality, an erotic union of sames.

While Sade and Illich speak to the same social symptom, loss of gender, their interpretations are exactly opposite. But that does not mean they are incompatible. It makes sense that a strong gender sensibility is possible only in relation to a strong feeling for genderlessness. The tendency to make sex abstract and the many pieties one hears about gender indicate that we suffer a split about the whole question. Gender talk quickly becomes propagandistic, simplistic, exaggerated, and divisive.

Patricia Berry offers further insights into the possible value of diminished gender. Her main argument is this: in childhood, to follow Freud's picture, the human being is polymorphous. Every part of the body offers pleasure. But for us to return to this polymorphous perversity is to get in touch with our inferiority. In that childlike sensuality, the adult also finds his shame and weakness. To avoid the inferiority of this pre-adult perversity, we turn to gender. We pursue opposites and thereby avoid the inferiority of a style before opposites. We get up from inferiority by repressing primal sexuality, turning instead into a highly sublimated culture of gender.

Berry goes on to say that gender becomes a primary metaphor by which we understand and articulate experience. But the trouble is, gender is an imprecise, broad-scaled metaphorical grid. A person reproaches himself saying: "I know why I did this; it's because I'm a man." Gender becomes dogma, and our perceptions of the world become too confined and too simplified.

Patricia Berry's solution to the problem of dogmatized gender is to return to the notion of gender some of the inferiority "genderism" serves to dispel. One example she gives concerns marriage. Marriage, she says, is generally too straight; it has all the repression of gender and little of the unexpected perversity of the child body. Couples complain that sexual experimentation doesn't have the thrill in marriage it had previously. Allowing childlike, inferior fantasy and feeling to have a place in marriage would soften the edges of gender and broaden the role of eros in this otherwise limited institution.

This analysis of gender as a defense against bodily and sexual inferiority fits well into the imagery of the Marquis de Sade. He not only presents sex as an inferior thing, full of the lowest, most perverted practices, but also in his writing style he gets his readers in touch with polymorphous perversity. Children can enjoy Sadeian talk about feces and asses and blood and gore. But adults take this absurd imagery with great seriousness and negativity, with intense feelings of righteousness. They ban his books. They don't see the moist humor in the perversity, as might an uncorrupted—that is, uncivilized and unsublimated—child. Sade's fiction, therefore, evokes the archetypal child, not the cute, well-behaved angel, but the primitive little one who might be caught playing with his feces or swearing up a storm.

A corollary to Sade's love of bottoms is the intensification of imagination implied in not looking at fronts. From that vantage point, anyone can be female, anyone male. It is all left to the imagination. Part of childlike polymorphous perversity is an intense imagining of the body. Sade's preference for the rear similarly turns from the literal to the imaginal. Sex therapy might in fact benefit from a Sadeian analysis of sexual activity since most problems presented in therapy are due to lack of imagination. If lovers could be both male and female in their lovemaking, maybe there would be less polarization: more feminine sensuality in the male, more masculine phallicism in the female.

The Gourmands of Excrement

Metaphoric attention to the backside brings us to a consideration of anality. Saturn's children spend their days shoveling excrement; they are "honey dippers," latrine workers. Sade quickly moves from the behind to excrement, inviting his readers once again to invert their tastes and sensibilities and arrive at an appreciation for the materials cast out of the body.

The following is a dream reported by a young man who was deeply in love with a woman he saw as sweet and wonderful. The two of them are sitting on a sofa in her parents' home. He slips his hand under her dress and feels soft flesh. He is overtaken by the sweet passion of the moment, but suddenly he notices something unexpected. She has deposited something in his hand. The dream is reminiscent of the lines from Swift that serve as the epigraph of Norman O. Brown's writing on anality: "nor wonder how I lost my wits; oh! Caelia, Caelia, Caelia shits." Since *Caelia* means "heavenly," one thinks of

Jung's dream in which God lets fall a gigantic turd on the grand cathedral. Heaven shits, and so does the heavenly woman.

An analyst who works with the dreams of his patients day after day knows, as perhaps others do not, that dreams of excrement are so common, so frequently reported, with such extraordinary variation and detail that the eliminatory organs of the body seem to be a primary concern of the imagination. The psyche clearly is enamored, as was Sade, with the anus, with its temenos of the backside, with its peculiar musculature, and with its product. Psychology cannot avoid placing this imagery near the center of its concern. From this point of view, Sade's scatological tendencies are by no means perversions or absurd fetishes. They directly reflect the spontaneous tendency of the psyche to present images of excrement.

Again we are close to the child: Freud's child, whose creativity is contained in his interest in feces, and our own personal childhood with its stories of peeing and shitting. Adult consciousness moved by its Justine conscience feels above such filthy matters. Yet, time and again an extremely intellectual, moral, fastidious, clean, high-minded man or woman will confess sheepishly: "I dreamed last night that I was in a bathroom where the toilets were overflowing and I was surrounded by shit."

James Hillman's book on dreams, *The Dream and the Underworld*, includes a fascinating section on diarrhea and is written with a true Sadeian appreciation for excrement. He interprets feces lovingly:

> It feels like mere anarchy is loosed upon the world, and the wish is for nothing more than an enclosed and private space to take down one's pants. Like the northerner gone south, the long-dreamt, long-wished vacation is fulfilled in a toilet.

> The toilet as death of the wish, as death wish, as joke, place of the clown. . . . The great pile of interpretative ideas about feces, what shit is supposed to "mean" (the crap about shit) . . . is an embarrassment of riches.[4]

Sade takes a trip from France to Italy and of all possible delights recounts the wonderful backside of Aphrodite. He is a northerner gone south, gone south literally and imaginally. Hillman's point is important and Sadeian: there is indeed liberation in anality. Worshipers of the rear might well be called libertines. In a society that is undeniably tight-assed—a pointed description of a culture that has surrendered to a narrow brand of morality—anal dreams suggest carnival, a return to the flesh that has been repressed, a recovery of the shitty stuff that comes out of our mouths when we are being free with words, an appreciation for feelings, thoughts, fantasies, and wishes that pour out of the imagination when it is allowed a "vacation." Hillman alludes to Saturn's carnival in his paean to excrement: "The old King falls apart and shits like a baby—decomposition and creation at once: incontinence, humiliation, ridicule, from Saturn, lord of privies and underwear, to Saturnalia." (184) The dream lover in sexual embrace is given a prize. Shitty dreams are often pleasant, strangely beautiful, and, as in this case, rewarding.

Saturn is the lord both of the outhouse and of freedom, Saturnalia. He liberates from the restraints of a narrow morality defined by a deep Justine fantasy. From a Sadeian point of view, when we celebrate Justine publicly in mammoth reaction-formations, protesting our innocence loudly, we are only exhibiting our captivity in innocence and its impoverishment. Saturn's shit, so repressed as to be the primary coin of locker-room language, comes out only symptomatically and outrageously. Our cities are littered with his literal garbage, and our homes are teeming with the excrement of violent family emotions.

The mystery of excrement deepens when the dreams become even more vile and interesting. Not only do many, many people dream of it, they also, these truly fine individuals, dream of eating it. Occasionally one hears the expletive "Eat shit and die!"—a genuine Saturnine greeting. Sade, of course, turns this image into a rite and dares to picture the erotic lure this netherworld eating has to humans:

> Shit-hatred is unfailingly the mark of the simpleton, that you will admit; but need I tell you that there is such a thing as shit-connoisseurship, shit-gourmandise? No habit is more easily acquired than mard-savoring; eat one, delicious, eat another, no two taste exactly alike, but all are subtle and the effect is somewhat that of an olive. (*Juliette*, 163)

To the gryphon we are simpletons if we don't recognize the value of uglifying; to Sade we're simpletons if we hate shit. The issue here is not to "integrate" some dark, shadowy element into personality but rather to taste the shitty flavors of life. Jung's dream of God dropping a turd on the cathedral suggests that shit is divine, and indeed in his writings Jung also showed an appreciation for this delicacy. He, too, by the way, picks up the humor that so often accompanies talk of shit, the kind of wit we saw in Hillman's amplification of diarrhea.

In *Symbols of Transformation* Jung analyzes the fantasies of a young American woman, an analysis that leads him into a discussion of excrement. His initial comments bring to mind Patricia Berry's description of the polymorphous perversity of non-gender childhood. "So if a much venerated object is related," writes Jung, "by the unconscious to the anal region, we have to conclude that this is a way of expressing respect and attention."[5] He goes on to tell of a patient who had a fantasy of her father sitting on a toilet while people filed past greeting him effusively. A patient of his saw in fantasy a crucifix formed of excrement. Another told of her father who called to her when she was on the toilet: "Come out at once! Whatever are you doing?" "I'm doing a little cart and two ponies," she answered from her site of creativity. Jung also mentions a French-speaking father whose child had a habit when talking of cocoa to say "caca-au-lit" (bed), a form of cocoa-au-lait (milk) that Sade would have enjoyed.

What we have in all of this is a valuation of shit, associated with childhood and related to food. I once heard a dream in which the dreamer was walking in a lovely garden with his lover picking fruit off the trees, offering it to his companion, but the fruit turned out to be turds growing on the branches. The woman refused the "fruit." It was my impression that in their "illicit" relationship they were not willing to eat the shit that was its fruit. They knew it was there, of course, but they didn't take it into their mouths, didn't taste it and feed on it. This "fruit" might have been true nourishment for their souls. Another person dreamed that, when her lover arrived for dinner, she had something in her mouth and couldn't talk. It was shit, and surprisingly she thought it tasted quite good. This was someone who had great difficulty in social situations being straightforward with her thoughts and feelings.

This "communion of Saturn" is truly a strange rite. Since *shit* means "cut" or "split," the word suggests that eating shit is to taste those very things we have filtered out. For example, Joanna Macy, a Buddhist scholar, offers seminars in which her audiences are led to taste the despair they feel, but habitually deny, over the existence of nuclear weapons. Life under the bomb is shit. It's easy to forget and to dismiss from attention this horror of modern life. In his book on eros, F. Gonzalez-Crussi credits Sade for insisting that we recognize the horrors we perpetrate in the world with feigned innocence. In this sense, innocence is the refusal to taste the shit we have in our mouths.

Sade says as plainly as possible that we need to eat shit! We need to taste the excrement of our chosen diet, to notice the flavors of all the feces we put out into the world. In that shit is the seed of liberation which can be savored. Indeed, those artists and writers who dare to taste culture's excrement are gourmands of shit.

But in Hillman's view excrement is not just the repressed; it is the food of the underworld. It is "cut off" from the dayworld of literal events. The anus is the undermouth, the under-opening, as Bosch showed in his carnival paintings. It is the gateway to the country down under, like the cave through which Dante finds the bowels of hell. Sade is then a representative of Hades, and so it is only proper that his books have been banned in an upperworld that does not know that domain. He belongs in the dark corners of bookstores and under bedsprings where he won't be exposed to the light of day. If anyone should be read in the bathroom, it is Sade.

The psychological underworld is active with Sadeian themes. Hillman points out that in mythology underworld streams are often thick with excrement. What is unacceptable in life, something to get rid of or cure away, from an under-world perspective may be quite ordinary and wholesome, even tasty. Pain, failure, conflict, jealousy, envy, despair—these and other "negative" experiences may, in the lower realm of the soul, be a gourmand's delight. The soul itself has an apprecia-tion for this truly foreign cuisine.

Saturated with jealousy, we may need to take it in until its flavors come through. Depression, Saturn's gift, can be tasted, put in the mouth, swallowed. It is not surprising that lovers would dream of eating shit together. Love has its excremental component, and this, along with the more wholesome diet, has to be consumed.

On the other side, seeing excrement as what is filtered out, we may need to taste it in our ordinary pieties and moralisms. A person who is "full of shit" is someone who doesn't recognize and speak for the unpleasant side of life. He doesn't express his own negativity. He has no "excremental vision," to use N. O. Brown's phrase. Since he doesn't like shit and therefore represses it, out it comes as the return of the repressed in the form of polite nonsense.

Obviously Sade's comment on the taste of an olive is brimming with dark humor, but it is comedy with a point. Knowing the shitty flavors of our everyday activities, we might be spared the atrocities of innocence. As Gonzalez-Crussi says in praise of Sade's attacks on innocence: "Millions of men die unjustly, at the hands of other men, all the time. And our response to this is 'I know it, and that is quite sufficient. Enough said; spare me the gory details.'"[6]

The View from the Rear

When he traveled to Italy, going incognito at times with the ingenious alias Sado, fondling the backsides of sculptures wherever he found them, Sade may not have known that he was enacting a traditional rite of Aphrodite. She was sometimes pictured as a Goddess appreciative of her backside, which was traditionally considered something to be appreciated. She was called Kalliglautos, She of the Lovely Behind. One of her characteristic postures was *anasyrma*, the lifting of her dress to reveal her naked body *and* looking behind, over her shoulder, at her backside. Dances were performed to her in which women lifted their skirts. Marilyn Monroe's celebrated pose in which she stands over a blowing grate on a New York street is an anasyrmic gesture Sade would have loved. The unhappy comment of her husband, complaining that her underpants were showing, underscores the role of the traditional kalliglautos in the gesture.

The backside of anything has its own beauty: the backside of a shiny city or of an imposing building. The backside of a personality is often much more fascinating and likable than what is presented from the front. There is little libertinage in the fronts of people, most of whom are redeemed at their posteriors. Gossip and biography are delightful precisely when they expose the rear.

Nevertheless, we are a frontal society, making certain to show a good face. How often do we go to pains, in the style of Sade, to show a good derriere? Therapy is generally not much interested in the frontal facts a patient tells: the explanations, the interpretations, the canonic stories. Psychotherapy requires an appreciation for the backside, what usually goes unseen and unnoticed. Of course this interest is perverse.

Sade had an extraordinary "rear" sensibility:

> Your asses, Madames, cursorily glanced at a short while ago, must be more narrowly studied; kindly step forward one by one and offer those articles to our criticism. (*Juliette*, 685)

> The devout sectator of Sodom, what with his extreme apprehensiveness lest the anterior charms of a woman upset the illusion he was laboring to form, required that these attractions be screened so completely from his view that the possibility of even suspecting their existence be circumvented. . . . "The ass, Madame, the ass," said he, "and, I beseech you, nothing but the ass." (*Juliette*, 132)

Government has an enormous backside, yet it rarely if ever presents it to the public. Occasionally a president or congressman will "moon" the citizenry, disregarding the rule that only fronts are to be shown, blatantly skimming off some funds or making an outrageous political move. But generally government keeps its backside covered—"covert," it says. A Sadeian mentality, on the other hand, would admit to the pleasures it gets from attention to the backside, where deals are made, moneys paid, selfishness rewarded, narcissism rampant. "Cover the president's ass," his loyal aides say to each other.

How different political life might be if Sade were let out of prison. We would all confess to our love of the unseemly. The true nature of our erotic interests would be revealed. If we are going to be despots in fact, we could play the role in full dress instead of covering our intentions with the clothing of innocence. The speeches of politicians are full of Justine, while the burden of their practice is pure Coeur-de-fer. How curious it is that in Sade's own life, when he was a magistrate in the revolutionary government, he was considered too lenient. He even dismissed the case against his mother-in-law, who had been responsible for most of his imprisonment.

A Sadeian sensibility always begs, no matter what the situation is, "the ass, please, nothing but the ass." The analyst wants to know what is *behind* this addiction to food, this new love, this unexpected depression. Overt explanations, the stories we tell ourselves, the convincing theories we hear from others are often a front, an unintentional defense. It takes the Sadeian virtue of cruelty and a perverse habitual attention to backside motivations to know better what is going on. The backside is a way into consciousness.

What Sade suggests with the body metaphor of the rump is a particular type of vision. Our perspectives can be introverted, extraverted, and backsided. The backside is the Kalliglautos Venus and the pratfallen Priapos, sometimes considered the husband of Aphrodite. In both, the emphasis is on the derriere; both suggest an archetypal posture in the world. Neither Venus nor Priapos finds much place in the modern world, which has to keep its public act clean. Aphrodite does get some attention in "exotic dancing," and Priapos appears in the routines of stand-up comics, but these release the repressed otherwise given a limited place in society. It is probably no accident that Sade appears historically in the very heyday of the Enlightenment as an antidote to sterile culture.

The move to the backside, while comic, is nevertheless a painful transition away from the frontal charms of Venus. Nothing Sadeian is easy. If it is easy, it is not Sadeian. In all Sadeian activities, from a teacher giving a difficult test to a lover breaking up an affair, the emotional tone is torture. So, too, the backside metaphor is not an easy accommodation with the shadow side of life. It is the response to an erotic tug that is commonly repressed and a deep appreciation for that side of things that is not always beautiful or revered or understood. And, to a forward-looking society, it is an uncommon delight and an unnatural preference.

5.

Isolation and Confinement

A talented child appears on stage to play his cello. He has the body and mannerisms of a ten-year-old, but his instrument plays as though it is in the hands of a mature performer. The master of ceremonies asks his mother about the child. In the course of her attempts to explain his talent, she mentions that all his life the boy has been digging. For the past three years, he has been digging a hole in his back yard that is big enough for an adult to crawl into. The mother confesses that sometimes she is embarrassed and explains the digging as her child's search for fossils, but the truth is, she says, he digs for the digging. He is an unusual child. One day his talent for the cello appeared, without the usual period of development. One day a mysterious desire to dig came upon him, and it still hasn't let him go.

Although the boy's mother didn't make any connection between the great hole in her back yard and her son's musical ability, one wonders. At the very least we can ask: Is this child who is possessed by some common yet mysterious earth rite the kind of child who can be possessed by a muse? Are the angels of art to be found in the earth as well as among the clouds?

In *The Poetics of Space* Gaston Bachelard comments on

the cellar as an important underground imaginal place. "It is first and foremost the dark entity of the house, the one that partakes of subterranean forces. When we dream there, we are in harmony with the irrationality of the depths."[1] The cellar, he goes on, becomes "buried madness, a walled-in tragedy." He refers to Edgar Allan Poe's "The Cask of Amantillado" as a story that exploits "natural fears which are inherent to the dual nature of both man and house." We humans like to roam the sunny earth, but there is also something compelling about the underground: the subway, the cellar, the child's excavation in the back yard.

The dual nature of man and house embraces the upper-world of familiar life and the cellar that calls forth irrational fantasy and fear. Ordinarily a person becomes adept at an instrument through learning and practice. But this digging boy seems to have uncovered something less rational and less developmental. Are there, then, two sets of natural laws: one for the world of day and another for life underground? Musical talent itself is a curious blend of daytime learning and night-time possession.

Sade apparently knew something about these mysteries of the cellar. In his fiction the remote, entombed chateau or monastery and the heavily sealed dungeon serve as ideal sites for the rites organized so carefully by the bishops, dukes, and other masters of ceremony. His description of the monastery of St. Mary-of-the-Wood offers a good example of the degree of isolation sought by the libertines:

> Six thick enclosures rise to baffle all attempts to see this building from the outside, even were one to climb into the church's tower; the reason for this invisibility is simple: the

> pavilion hugs the ground. Its height does not attain twenty-five feet, and the compounded enclosures, some stone walls, others living palisades formed by trees growing in strait proximity to each other, are, all of them, at least fifty feet high. . . . This pavilion has, in all, nothing but basements, a ground floor, an entresol, a first floor; above it there is a very thick roof covered with a large tray, lined with lead, filled with earth, and in which are planted evergreen shrubberies. (*Justine*, 579)

Nothing but basements. Bachelard tells about a dreamer whose chateau had a "cluster of cellars for roots." "What power it gave," he says, "that simple house."

The power and the fear of the cellar or dungeon are chthonic. Reason, on a plane with the surface of life, has its own kind of power and even its own fears. But chthonic places evoke a particular imagination that is not the same as that of ordinary life. *Chthon* signifies earth, the place of burial (*Iliad*, 6. 411), and the earth as a Goddess (Aeschylus, *Eumenides*, 6). It is also a land or country. The word is related to the Hittite *tegan*, ground, and Iranian *du*, place.[2] There is an atmosphere to chthon that is not at all the same as that of surface life. It is the atmosphere one feels climbing down into a dark basement or walking through an old cemetery, especially at night. It is an atmosphere alien and threatening to the world of light with which we typically identify. Yet, it, too, as Bachelard says, is part of our nature.

In Sade the important chthonic setting is shielded from the sunny sky as a sharp contrast to the heavenly focus of his contemporaries and their enlightenment. Sade speaks for the earthy demands of the soul, and he speaks in language appropriate to that place, concentrating on its blood, its slime, its earthworm point of view. His style, as well as the burden of his stories, is chthonic.

A house or a person may have a dual nature, upper and lower, but that doesn't imply that the two work well together. Turn over a rock, and the earthworm will shy away from light and retreat into his earth. Daily life moves along fine without frequent intrusions from the chthonic places. Chthon, for its part, requires protection from the bright light of day. Like vampires who can't withstand the piercing rays of the sun, chthonic figures shield themselves from all things solar. So, Sade goes to lengths to provide his libertines with their necessary isolation from ordinary bright-minded society.

Sade's description of St. Mary-of-the-Wood emphasizes its invisibility to the casual passerby or even to someone intent on seeing it from a church tower. Church-tower consciousness won't catch a glimpse of what Sade and his libertines are doing. In ordinary life, too, it is difficult to notice our own Sadeianism in raising children, making laws, carrying out the penalties of justice, or waging just wars. Yet, chthonic strains are there, rationalized with warm, shining reasons. We execute criminals in order to deter crime; we make multi-kiloton bombs to prevent nuclear war; our benign intelligence agencies spy on ordinary citizens for the sake of national security. Our reasons are enlightened, but our methods are dark and not as unrelated to Sade's imagination as we might hope.

The Sadeian necessities of life can also be camouflaged by scapegoating, so that we see libertinage only in criminals or in political enemies. Paradoxically, when we scapegoat or project the Sadeian elements on others, we enter into our own sadism. We murder criminals with impunity. When we think we have seen a despicable Sadeian political character in the world, we call out the armed forces. We don't see libertinage clearly because we look from church towers or from citadels of reason, and we fail to understand criminality because we are unconsciously identified with the sadist.

Like the trees that hide Sade's remote monastery, there are certain natural protections that allow Sadeian activities to take place without penalty. Humor, for example, is an effective natural cover. Hollywood makes a comedy called *How to Murder Your Wife*, and nobody raids the cinemas for telling a sadistic story or corrupting the morals of our youth.

Sade recognized that natural impediments are not sufficient to protect the precincts of the libertine. The monastery is fitted with a roof of lead, Saturn's metal, making a thick, heavy, impenetrable shield against the light of day. Isolation from values of the sky and ordinary reason allow for a kind of morality and virtue altogether unknown in a world governed in the light.

Teachers often like to do their work in classrooms where the door can be closed, not because of anything literally improper that might go on and not just out of personal insecurity, but because teaching is a Sadeian endeavor. It requires isolation from an ordinary mentality. The same is true of psychotherapy. The consulting room—its privacy usually well protected naturally by doors and ritually by leaden, Saturnine rules and schedules—is the scene of libertinage. There a client will reveal chthonic aspects of his or her nature. The closed room is not only a vessel of containment, it is also a shielded place where the dark stuff of the soul can pour out without being contaminated by the light of normal values.

Sade's further descriptions of the monastery give a better idea of the psychological isolation required for certain Sadeian activities:

> Nothing inflames them, nothing stimulates their imagination like the impunity guaranteed them by this impregnable retreat, certain never to have other witnesses to their excesses than the very victims they feast upon, sure indeed their perversities will never be revealed, they carry them to the most abhorrent extremes; delivered of the law's restraints, having burst the checks Religion imposes, unconscious of those of remorse, there is no atrocity in which they do not indulge themselves. . . . Nothing incenses them . . . like impunity. (*Justine*, 580)

The most cherished ideas and values of enlightened life threaten chthonic perception. Libertines are liberators of imagination, freeing it from the impositions of civilized thought. Sade shows that we have an erotic attraction to the lower, darker places and to activities proper to that underground place. But in order for these unfamiliar erotic movements to be fulfilled, we have to do something about the assumptions, interpretations, habits of thought, and moral limits that civilization and reason impose or insinuate. From a chthonic point of view, civilization is a form of repression.

Enlightenment not only blinds us to the typical ugly necessities of a Sadeian world; more subtly it keeps us apart from imagination altogether. The trouble with most dream analysis and literary criticism is that they "civilize" images that by nature, like Bachelard's house, have a chthonic component. Therefore, artists, and dreamers too, put up "thick walls" around their images in order to keep dangerous civilizing interpretations away. Samuel Beckett, when pressed to offer meanings for his plays, always said something like: "No meanings where none intended."

If thick walls are not enough, then a wide, deep, threatening moat may be in order. Artists isolate themselves, making themselves islands in the sea of society (*isolation* is from the Latin *isola*, island) in order to protect their imaginations and their works. Leonardo's biographer Heydenreich says of him: "The inner reserve, the impersonality of his nature, must have been so great as to form an insurmountable barrier between himself and others—a barrier which neither he nor others could cross."[3] Imagination is particularly vulnerable to so-called "reality," to the mistaken notion of enlightenment that its ways are the only ways, that reason knows best. For all its romanticism, there is something Sadeian, too, in Thoreau's retreat at Walden Pond.

The libertine loves remote spots that the world passes by. Ridolfi, Tintoretto's biographer, describes the painter's isolation: "He spent most of his time withdrawn in his studio which was situated in the remotest part of the house, where his occupation required a light to burn all day long. . . . He would rarely admit any but servants there, not even friends, let alone other artists, nor did he ever let other painters see him at work."[4] Notice the typical Sadeian tone of cruelty in these efforts toward isolation. We feel a person's attachment to Sadeian values as an affront to enlightened virtues of community, sociability, and geniality. Sadeian acts in favor of liberty "wound" civilized sensibilities of the psyche. Sade wounds a sense of propriety, but again, just as narcissism is deepened by its being wounded, conventionality and propriety can find soul in a Sadeian attack.

People perform Sadeian rituals of isolation in the most ordinary contexts, closing out ordinary life both internally and externally. A person will go off on a trip alone or shut himself in a room. Slamming a door in anger and frustration is a familiar Sadeian rite that benefits the soul by granting it its seclusion.

People around feel the Sadeian sting of these isolating actions, and the slammer, though he may deny it, enjoys the pleasures of his solitude, true Sadeian delight in being away from family and society. The sentiment of a husband or wife enjoying some time away from each other and the children usually is expressed in jokes, but the feeling is real. If marriage is taken sentimentally, this Sadeian virtue of isolation can go underground and become a plaguing desire. Claims for solitude do not imply an absolute withdrawal of love, but they do speak for dark, cold, chthonic requirements of the soul that lie at the very heart of love, marriage, and community.

Civilization's repressed Sadeianism comes out in all kinds of tortures. Prisons, schools, courts, police departments—they all fall into literal expressions of sadism. National community takes the form of torturous taxes, laws, and oppressions. Society bent on "community" investigates the slightest deviations from normalcy. In the United States the FBI keeps records on writers who dare to explore any human conditions that challenge only slightly the narrow band of values expressly approved by the society's laws. Ignorant of certain Sadeian requirements, society professes an innocent ideal, while it enforces sadistic avenues toward a smooth-running community.

Libertines have reason to worry about retribution and punishment; they seek a place where they can let their imaginations roam in their peculiar directions without punishment. We tend to think of pragmatism and literalism as the main enemies of imagination, but another challenge is the moral antagonism that sees fantasy, dream, and image as contrary to values of work and truth or that wants to judge images as good and appropriate. Imagination doesn't need new ideas and cleverness nearly as much as it needs freedom from persecution.

If there is any cruelty inherent in the work of the artist, it is the effort needed to keep imagination unfettered. Civilization hesitates to allow imagination to roam freely. That freedom has to be achieved, as in the case of the artists mentioned above, who to some extent spurned society and family. But this effort on behalf of imagination is not only something for artists; it is also for the soul-caretaker in anyone. We all have to become cruelly Sadeian to protect our images and our imaginations.

For example, a woman filled with a desire to spend a year abroad goes to a therapist. She has a dependent husband and a job that keeps the family living well. The therapist could take a civilized point of view and help his patient see that her responsibilities lie with her family. Or, he could withstand the cruelty in her vision and support it as a force working on behalf of her imagination. To protect this uninvited fantasy may require a ruthless attitude toward ordinary duties. It may batter the sensitivities of her loved ones. Imagination does not always soothe the worries of everyday life.

Roland Barthes describes Sadeian isolation as an effort to "shelter vice from the world's punitive attempts."[5] Barthes's comparison of Sade's libertine retreats with Loyola's spiritual exercises runs deep. A monk takes to the monastery to protect his virtue, the libertine to safeguard his vice.

An analyst often finds himself in the position of protecting a person's vice. Vice, of course, is relative. For example, it is quite common for a person to believe strongly in the virtue of selflessness. Many of us have been brought up in the absolute certainty that selfishness is a vice. But when you listen to the life stories of a selfless person, you hear bitterness about that virtue, and you notice typical signs of repression. The selfless person is often subtly controlling and self-serving. Attention to self has gone underground, not to Sade's carefully arranged chthonic chambers of vice, but to places of repression. The analyst thinks: Why couldn't this person give some honest, straightforward attention to himself, instead of disclaiming self-responsibility in the name of selflessness? "It's too easy for me to be selfish," such a person will say, blind to the narcissism in his beloved virtue. Here is a case in which some training in Sadeian self-centeredness might correct extravagant virtue.

The Sadeian Misfit

Retreating from society, externally or internally, is one way to find freedom for imagination, but imagination also needs an escape from the lure of civilized values. The Bohemianism of artists is one way out of the pressing enticements of normal life: comfort and dullness, forgetfulness, and a drowsy acceptance of the status quo as if it were absolute truth. Therefore, artists sometimes take a Sadeian approach to society for the sake of imagination.

In the April, 1964, issue of *Playboy*, Jean Genet describes his isolation in prison. His story is remarkably similar to Sade's experience of confinement. Genet tells how he wrote the beginning of a book on paper that was intended for making paper bags. One day he returned to his cell to find his "book" missing, and he was punished for not using the paper properly. "I felt belittled by the warden's robbery. I ordered some notebooks at the canteen, got into bed, pulled the covers over my head and tried to remember, word for word, the fifty pages I had written. I think I succeeded." Two hundred years before, Sade had written *120 Days of Sodom* on a single roll of paper thirteen yards long and five inches wide, both sides covered with microscopic handwriting. This manuscript, too, to Sade's despair, was lost. It was not recovered until after his death.

Genet's story tells the triumph of imagination over the oppression of society, but it also gives a deeper clue to the way imagination works. The ritual of writing on paper bags takes the writing away from the intentions and the comfortable designs of civilization. This Sadeian crime and breaking of prison rules support Genet's persona as a criminal in service of imagination. Writing furtively on paper bags, like Sade's toilet-paper scribbling, sustains the fiction in which the writer serves his muse of the prison cell.

In these similar stories of Sade and Genet, Saturn appears once again, this time in the form of constriction. A composer I know once told me about a piece for handbells he was commissioned to write. He had just begun to sketch the composition and work up some thematic and harmonic materials for it when he received a call from his patron informing him that the handbell society lacked means and didn't have an A-flat bell. The composer had been writing the piece in E-flat, which would normally absolutely require the A-flat. But, given the restriction, he wrote a fascinating work. Necessity is often Sadeian, but imagination can flourish in constricting poverty as well as in riches. In his fiction Sade praised wealth, but the only wealth he enjoyed with any consistency was the inexhaustibility of his imagination.

Along similar lines, Genet responds to his interviewer who had commented on Genet's sparse life. "Mine is the poverty of angels," he says, "I just don't give a damn about possessions and the like. . . . What need have I for objects and luxury? I write, and that's enough. . . . Most of our activities have the vagueness and vacantness of a tramp's existence. We very rarely make a conscious effort to transcend that state. I transcend it by writing."

Genet's poverty, like that of the monk, is elected. Sade's was imposed. But the effect is the same. Withdrawal from society's values leaves the imagination free to create. There is little difference between the monasticism of the saint, of the modern writer, and of the pervert: each takes a vow of poverty. One is always practicing monasticism when one is isolating oneself, paring life down to essentials, finding a remote, well-protected place for reverie. This monastic move may not be literal; it may take the form of merely clearing off a desk. But as a Sadeian rite it puts civilization off to the side for the sake of imagination. Marsilio Ficino taught "When the external act decreases, the internal act is strengthened." Decreasing the external act, however, is often an affront to society, the act of a libertine.

Genet is clear about the relationship between the constriction of his life and his literary output. After Jean-Paul Sartre's book *Saint Genet* appeared, Genet's life deteriorated. "I remained in that awful state for six years, six years of the imbecility that's the basic stuff of life: opening a door, lighting a cigarette. There are only a few gleams in a man's life. All the rest is grayness. But this period of deterioration made for a meditation that led me finally to the theater."

What looks like deterioration may be a kind of interiorization. Genet's confinement and poverty directed him to imagination, to writing for the theater, to a form of expression that contains much of what he found in the dark brooding of his isolation. It is remarkable how often the greatest works of imagination portray the darkness and aggression that are more indigenous to the prison than to free society: the *Iliad*, the *Odyssey*, the Bible, *Tristan and Isolde*—they all present the human condition with an accent on its warfare, trials, sufferings, and poisons. Even comedy, especially comedy, holds much of what Sade revered. The violence of Punch and Judy and of the Three Stooges and the everyday disasters of Laurel and Hardy show the violence that is in nature and in the human heart with a comic tone less dark and less subtle than Sade's. The Sadeian slap of life is funny because at least it shows the hand of God outwitting human intention and will.

Sade's Negative Way

James Hillman's essay on the negativity of the senex considers our problem of Saturn in the light, or dark, of medieval alchemy and Renaissance art.[6] Hillman finds a purpose in the negative qualities of Saturnine moods and behaviors. Certain dark spots of the heart, he says, can only be perceived by dark methods. "Hatred, envy, grinding meanness become tools of insight. They provide ways of darkening the light and cutting deeply into psychological truth. By dimming the brightness and by hiding and cloaking the head, depression also wraps and cares for the soul."[7] Hillman is referring here to the iconographic tradition in which Saturnine people are pictured with their heads in their hands or wearing broad-brimmed hats shading their faces. In Sade this idea takes the form of underground isolation, a misanthropic hiding from the world, covering the top with lead, hiding one's facial identity by taking a number rather than a name.

A negative withdrawal from the world, whether in monk-like seclusion or in moods of depression, leads to a place where there is no positive valuation to limit the meandering of imagination. As Hillman says, it leads to an emptiness in which imagination can stir, unshackled by narrow-minded judgments. In this light, Sade's St. Mary-of-the-Wood is not really a parody of religion; it is a further revelation of what religion and monasticism are all about. The strict rules of the monastic day, or the regimen of prison, obviously limit life. But they also give it form, turning time and the habits of ordinary life into objects for aesthetic contemplation, releasing imagination in a way that ordinary unstructured life cannot.

This negativity of the Sadeian way may seem so revolting, of course, that a person will avoid it at all costs. Indeed, the price sometimes is a division within the soul. When the Sadeian necessity is not given its due, it tends to split into absurd versions of itself. The person not mean enough to isolate himself in a Sadeian manner may actually withdraw affection in his life, not aware of the violence in his act, and, on the other side, suffer masochistic loneliness. Some people obsessed with community and sharing and togetherness find isolation a moral fault; yet, these same people can be incapable of intimacy, their Sadeian potential turned into sadistic coldness and distance.

A young woman, mother of two children, wife of a successful financial broker, mistress of a conventionally affluent household, meticulous in carrying out her social obligations, has the following dream. She is imprisoned in a cell that looks out on a green, grassy meadow. She feels the incarceration as torture, as a tantalizing denial of that "peaceable kingdom" on the far side of the bars. She experiences the dream as a nightmare.

It's a puzzling dream, since in actual life the dreamer lives on the side of the fence where the grass really *is* greener. Someone not educated in the mysteries of Sade might think nevertheless that the dreamer is repressed and needs to find her way to a better life. However, a Sadeian view of the dream suggests that the dreamer fortunately—*felix culpa*—finds herself in prison, cut off from green life, isolated and therefore on a path toward a deeper, darker way of imagining. Here she has an opportunity to withdraw from the burdens of her success and the limits of her green, carefree existence.

It is not unusual to come upon people whose outward lives look comfortable and fulfilled and whose inward feelings are tortured. An appreciation for Sade might give that torture an interior room where it can do its work. Sade's hatred of convention and sentimentality is not just personal misanthropy. It is a positive recognition of the dangers of pleasantness taken to the extreme and made into a rule. Sade's leather straps reflect as in a mirror the ways in which the conventional world can handcuff a life.

Familiar green values of growth, relationship, and youthful idealism simply have no place in Sade's settings. His way is dark. Hillman remarks: "Crucial to this move into internal space is realizing that it must be black and must be empty, otherwise the antidote cannot appear in the poison."[8] Take the poison out of Sade, and you lose his bitter healing herb.

Reading his novels, you get the impression that Sade is continually pushing his vision to the limit. Civilization offers strong resistance to anyone searching for a dark alternative. Sade obviously makes a strong effort to keep his viewpoint consistent. In *Juliette* he says of nature: "There is but one way to make her bare her secrets, through incessant, unwearying study of her; only by probing into her furthermost recesses may one finally destroy the last of one's misconceptions." In this sense the author's imaginal exploration of the dark is one with the efforts of his characters, the libertines, to explore the dark potential of the human heart. One's "misconceptions" are those ideas and ideals put forward by enlightened society or, more deeply, by that bias in the psyche that favors enlightened understanding and glowing values.

The honesty in this Sadeian program chills the heart, and resistance against the negative way is indeed strong. Patients in analysis faced with some pressing inner developments often think that it is enough to go halfway with them. The person committed to exploring the heart will often draw a boundary line for the therapy. The psyche, however, always demands more than we expect.

Psychologists often practice the conventional wisdom: a person suffering a strong impact of the soul should keep a grip on mundane reality. Much of modern psychotherapy applies this humanistic treatment to patients suffering delusions and florid fantasy. Sade, however, moves on without looking back. Daring the emptiness and the inversion of values that come with open exploration of the heart, he aims at complete isolation from cherished convention. In his honesty he offers a ritual of imagination that goes against all accepted notions of health and morality. Yet, perhaps there lies, in Hillman's words, the antidote in the poison, a homeopathic remedy that meets our actual tendencies toward violence and sociopathy with images equal to our behavior.

Sadeian isolation is a turn away from the values that paradoxically lend support to cruel behavior. Turning away from these conventional values means moving toward their opposites, but in imagination, not in literal action. By taking Sade seriously, we bring our antisocial behavior into a proper imaginal context and give our ills the imagination they lack. Literalism, the only real disease, is lack of appropriate imagination. The value of Sade's literary creations is that they give a mythic background to the violence of the heart. In this way

Sade is a doctor of the soul, treating our loneliness, our violence, and our various forms of dehumanization with homeopathic images, with scenarios of mythic proportions that unveil the darkly ominous themes hiding behind cheery rationalizations.

Isolation fulfilled is individuation. When we cannot see the basement of our souls from our chosen roost in the church belfry, then that part of the soul is free to manifest itself. There is movement toward becoming what we are in relation to fate, rather than what we wish to be from a pleasant but limited point of view. When actual isolation does its work, that isolation is taken inward to become individuality. Therefore, this Sadeian virtue, achieved and protected with aggression, allows the soul to coalesce into character. If the isolation is merely symptomatic—everyone dashing to the suburbs to avoid community—then there will be no community. But if isolation moves the soul toward its unique fate, then a community of individuals can arise. Without individuals who have been fashioned by isolation, what we call community is only a collective. Paradoxically, then, Sade's strong advocacy of the well-protected hide-out is not literal misanthropy. It is service to the soul, and only from the soul can genuine community arise.

6.
Black Humor

Like a walk through a cow pasture, reading Sade requires a certain delicacy of approach. Read him up close, and you are liable to dismiss him as a dirty old crank. Stand back a few inches, however, letting in some light, allowing metaphor and imagination, and Sade appears less as a pervert and more as a novelist of conviction. Exactly the right distance and angle, moreover, reveal Sade the humorist.

Certainly if there is humor in Sade it is black humor, so black at times as to require a strong effort of imagination to appreciate the joke at the heart of his vision. His attacks on religion will wound one's faintest attachment to theology, and yet humor adds a spice to Sade's project of turning the world inside out. For example, Juliette finds it quite a challenge to corrupt a pious Spaniard, but she has little difficulty once she has placed three young boys in his way. "Man is weak," she comments. "The pious are weaker than most, especially when you offer them boys. Seldom sufficiently stressed, often not even realized, there exists a powerful analogy between believers in God and buggers." (*Juliette*, 630)

Most would agree that this "powerful analogy" has indeed escaped the notice of religious people. Sometimes Sade's humor comes from absurd conjunctions such as this. We might call it a "dark oxymoron": God and buggers. Yet within the absurdity is a serious, depressing truth: piety—so vulnerable to superficiality, often achieved with superhuman and artificial championing of innocence, and tending toward masochistic self-denial—easily turns into its opposite. The strange truth is that it is the pious person, the normal person, the respectable person who often turns savage, as though the very insistence on and cultivation of frontal values set up a person for behavior that is turned around, darker, and secret.

Sade is especially the humorist when he offers his inverted reasoning with all the seriousness of philosophic rhetoric, but with a conclusion that is absurd and revolting. In *Justine*, for example, Rodin gives a long oration on the moral basis for killing children.

> One has the power to take back what one has given; amongst no race that has ever dwelled upon earth has there been any disputing the right to dispose of one's children as one sees fit. . . . Several passages in the pentateuch prove that amongst the children of God one was allowed to kill one's children; and, finally, God Himself ordered Abraham to do just that. It was long believed, declares a celebrated modern author, that the prosperity of empires depends upon the slavery of children; this opinion is supported by the healthiest logic. (553)

Offering a scriptural defense for killing children is also a creative piece of theology in the tradition of the feast of fools. The imagery of dreams and literature tends to be quite powerful and larger than life. Stated so plainly in Sade, the slavery of children may sound shocking and absurd. But his imagery may not be far removed from one of the shadows of parenthood.

Parents do in fact feel, although they would probably rarely admit it, the kind of mastery and dominion over their children that is well-imaged in Sade's language of slavery and cannibalism.

The parent–child relationship is one of those primary settings in which sado-masochism flourishes. But it flourishes there because a genuine form of mastery and dependence is entirely appropriate. Child-rearing requires authority and power on the part of the parent and a certain level of submission in the child. When this Sadeian arrangement is accepted, there should be few problems. But when it is denied, an overlay of sentimental values concerning family may be completed with an underlay of actual sado-masochism. A soulful family structure would include strong exercise of power and heartfelt submission. This differs entirely from "splitting the archetype," in which family violence erupts from a failure to embrace and contain family power patterns.

Another example from *Juliette* has the pope, no less, commenting on the various ways in which the saints were martyred. Obviously this is good material for Sade, combining religion and torture. "We see St. Catherine bound," says the pope, "to a nail-studded cylinder and rolled down a mountainside. Now there, Juliette, is a pleasant way of getting to heaven, don't you agree?" (795) Sade's sarcasm and sardonic humor in the face of religion's piety is obvious; what better foil for a devotee of sado-masochism than religion. But Sade also pointedly highlights a sado-masochistic preoccupation in religion that sees virtue in being tortured. Religions seem to have no trouble getting people to submit their wills and wallets to the severe demands of pious authorities. Showing a great variety of tortures, medieval illuminated books glory in the martyrdom of St. Catherine. Sade picks up on this masochistic element in religion, the tendency to endure anything for eternal rewards.

In a footnote to the pope's comment on St. Peter, Sade pokes irreverent fun at a figure who is rarely the butt of a joke: Jesus. In this passage the pope is making a scholarly remark on the word-play in the name of St. Peter. Sade notes: "Whence the pun made by Jesus, that imbecile who, as everyone knows, never opened his mouth but riddles, anagrams, or puzzles came out of it. His talk is all tedious allegory, where places are joined on to names, names to places, and the facts always sacrificed to illusions." (749) Sade sounds like a stand-up comic making a living, as many Sadeian comedians do, with irreverent pokes at the noblest of figures.

Here Sade engages in some daring humor as part of his attempt to soil religion. Black humor blackens. It takes those very things we consider white and sacred and places them outrageously in a different context. Whereas most biblical scholars would spend their lives seriously examining the figures of speech found everywhere in the New Testament texts, usually with the idea of making a positive contribution to theology, Sade brings out the shadow in biblical circumlocutions. He caricatures the difficulty they present to anyone who wants to know clearly the pristine message of this religion that has been open to many contrasting interpretations and yet has been the basis of culture for two millennia. To the illusion that Christianity presents a clear way of life to its devotees, Sade offers a shadowy reconsideration.

One of the functions of humor, especially black humor, is to unlock the shadow from its imprisonment in some pious belief. Joy often accompanies this liberation. Laughter often has a dark rim. Rarely has Christian theology been critical of the obscurity of its inherited texts. Rarely does it celebrate the foolishness of elaborating such a finely structured theology and religious life from such a small and obscure source. Christianity has many such shadows which, with a Sadeian touch, might open hidden reservoirs of religious insight.

A solid criticism of Christianity, parodied here in Sade, might release shadow in a positive way, allowing this religion its irrationality and extremes. Theology might learn from Sade that the priesthood is also a clownship, an absurd posture that derives some of its power directly from its absurdity. We all believe, when we truly believe, with Tertullian, because our belief is absurd. Sade's pope is an unbelievably coarse, obnoxious, immoral caricature. But in a sense this pope is the absolute apogee of religion's shadow and therefore is as sacred and as important as any romanticized notion of papacy. If we make the pope a paragon of purity, then we need Sade's "Unholy Father" in order to be saved from absolute lopsided naivete.

The Bile in Sadeian Humor

"Black Humor" is a classical term much discussed in medieval philosophy and medicine. In the theory of humors, the melancholic humor is identified with bile and labeled "black." So, black humor is itself a pun which suggests, if taken seriously, that the biting, sardonic tone in Sade's wicked mirth might have something in common with the ancient, sophisticated medical theory of the melancholic humor.

Saturn and Melancholy, the extraordinary study by the art historians Klibansky, Panofsky, and Saxl of the long tradition surrounding melancholy and genius, demonstrates that the black humor is traditionally both poison and elixir. It can be both a passing affliction and a lifelong temperament. It leads to a life of dryness, sadness, depression, and inactivity; yet it is also a source of exalted genius and inspiration. The authors cite Marsilio Ficino describing both the profundity and illumination that melancholy provides. In Ficino's words, the black humor "obliges thought to penetrate and explore the 'centre' of its objects, because the black bile is itself akin to the centre of the earth. Likewise it raises thought to the comprehension of the highest, because it corresponds to the highest of the planets."[1]

Sade's imaginal journey is a trip to the center of the earth. He abjures travel out to the planets, convinced apparently that there is a measure of insight to be found in the dark center that few have explored. Given a choice between the light of day and the dark interior, Sade always chooses the sealed chamber, the remote hideaway, or an underground crypt.

Dependent on this black humor, Sade's writing shows traces of both sides of it. It is dry, cold, dark, bitter, scatological, critical, and sardonic—all qualities of black bile's patron, Saturn. But it also less obviously aims at a brutally honest view of human capacity, a fully enlightened investigation of the most cherished cultural institutions, and a search for the very roots of the human attraction to evil. The black humor reveals what the lighter humors cannot penetrate. Sade achieves his perspective with dark means, but it may take a blackened eye to see the dark delights of the heart.

Humor in general shares some of the ambivalent qualities of black bile. It can seek out the shadow in any institution without literally opposing that institution. It is a form of catharsis that breaks through the usual defenses, revealing some element we would rather keep covered. So, humor is at once a blackening, when that is its method, and a whitening. The whitening is achieved directly through the blackening, as in an alchemical process in which heat presses black soot into white ash. Jung described the process of self-knowledge as a delving into black melancholy:

> Self-knowledge is an adventure that carries us unexpectedly far and deep. Even a moderately comprehensive knowledge of the shadow can cause a good deal of confusion and mental darkness, since it gives rise to personality problems which one had never remotely imagined before. For this reason alone we can understand why the alchemists called their *nigredo* melancholia, "a black blacker than black," night, an affliction of the soul, confusion, etc., or, more pointedly, the "black raven."[2]

Nigredo, blackening, gives rise to Sade's entire enterprise, a literature full of personality problems, afflictions, confusion, and mental darkness. His way is to be blacker than black, not only in the staging of sexual scenarios, but also in the dark humor that chars the whitest of values and institutions. We have little trouble imagining the purity of absolute whitening and clarity, but we seem to miss the possibility of finding an anti-clarity, a perception so brilliantly black that the interiority of whatever is under question shines forth. Opposite to innocent white perception is a pure, dark epiphany, an appearance of meaningfulness that captures the essence of the shadow that has been neglected and repressed in the white search for meaning. The Sadeian imagination heads off for this dark pole at the center of things, certain to find a focus of intelligibility.

Naturally Sade selects the whitest objects for his black humor: children, religion, family, innocence. The bite of his "black raven" stings with special pain because he goes directly to the heart of innocence and purity—to our very love of children, for instance—and coldly justifies the horrendous abuse of those innocents. But isn't that the nature of our problem with child abuse? Parents subject children every day to unimaginable torture, and they do it in a culture that romanticizes the child. If we were to take an unbiased look at the place of the child in modern Western society, we would see a split attitude: on one hand parents try to give their children everything possible, with fantastic Walt Disney images of childhood, while on the other hand parents also dominate, bind, torture, and sexually abuse those sentimentalized children. As repugnant as Sade's humor around the abuse of children is, it suggests a liberation into consciousness of those terrible loves and horrendous attractions: the genuine, undeniable human desire to dominate children and to fulfill some erotic demand with them. Here is an exceedingly dark truth, a center-of-the-earth reality that clearly we would rather avoid facing. It deeply offends a powerful affection for the child. Yet, as Sade might say, these bad things happen in the world and therefore, in some way, they partake of a shockingly dark reality.

Only the raven knows what opaque mystery lies in the widespread desire to hurt and love unnaturally those children whose innocence we cherish. What Sade presents in his absurd philosophy and anthropology is a darkly humorous affirmation of that desire. Rather than look for something malfunctioning in odd and destructive loves of children, Sade searches out a positive attraction to the evil that is the genuine seed of abuse.

Recognizing that we find the archetypal child in actual children, we could explore this hatred and love of the child. We have already seen that innocence calls for torturous deepening and maturing. Could it be that we cannot let the archetypal child submit to maturing processes, so we act out those repressed initiations in our brutality? At the root of his outrageous statements in support of child abuse, Sade suggests that there is indeed a universal truth in that torture. The child requires abandonment by the parents.

I once heard a dream of a woman who in life was excessively devoted to her children. In the dream she had her children lying on a table in front of her. At her side was a cart filled with a variety of sharp, ugly knives. Her task was to cut her children into pieces. She awoke from the dream terrified and guilty. But it seemed to me that this dream was very much like the passages of Sade about children; it expressed in image a truth about being a parent, the ugly fact that a parent has to be strong, at times depriving, and often unreasonably and laceratingly sharp. This mother could not let her children go unprotected. Of course, the pattern had a deeper level within the mother herself. It was the eternal Child that she protected so fiercely, a child that had been penned in throughout her life by the restrictive values of her own father and later within the strict confines of her religious morality. We abuse children because we do not want the archetypal child to be subjected to the torments of initiation.

If this mother could find distance and humor, she might learn something important from Sade's absurd philosophy of childhood. Her dream itself is either horror story or black comedy or both. On one level it shows what she is doing to the archetypal child—brutalizing it, cutting it into pieces. It also indicates the subterranean ways she is torturing her actual children through compulsive protectiveness. Finally, it shows her what she might have to do at a deep level: cut into that child complex that has her locked in a mother–child vise.

In another image Sade suggests that the child needs to be transformed and internalized. As usual his imagery is rather concrete. Juliette is visiting the completely uncivilized giant Minski. He is serving his guests an extraordinary dinner of human flesh.

> "We'll try some," said Sbrigani; "it is absurd to turn up one's nose at anything . . . it is no more extraordinary, after all, to eat a human than to eat chicken."
>
> So saying my husband dug his fork into a joint of boy which looked to him especially well prepared. (*Juliette*, 585)

Child-eating may be a way of internalizing and tasting childhood and the archetypal child. There is something about romanticizing the child and keeping him or her fixed, unaffected, and unmoved that is masochistic. Internalizing the child requires aggression. Any identification with childhood is a masochistic avoidance. Appropriating the child, however, allowing the child to have a place, even in adult life, requires strength, standing up to the adult world that denigrates childhood while romanticizing it. We may need to appreciate the "flavor" of the child and truly "incorporate" it. Something in the soul may well have a taste for "joint of boy."

Again, James Hillman offers an important reflection on our treatment of the child. He points out a vicious circle: "Abandoning *of* the child in order to become mature and then abandonment *to* the child when it returns. Either we repress or we coddle this face of our subjectivity. In both cases the child is unbearable."[3] In adulthood we cannot bear the dependency, the body, the desire, the polymorphous perversity, the naivete, the imagination of the child. The Sadeian imagination sees this repression and offers absurd, comic images of taking that child back in.

Sade also portrays our need and love of the archetypal child, repressed in a heroic adult society and therefore acted out in symptoms of abuse. We long for the perceived freedom and imagination of the child, and that repressed longing gets transformed into guilt-ridden sexual liaisons.[4] We crave the child, and yet we do everything to avoid the inferiority that is attached to what we crave. Sade's man decides to give "joint of boy" a try; after all, it's like chicken. It's similar, that is, to other things we incorporate, and so there is no need for disgust.

The Flow of the River Styx

David L. Miller offers an extraordinary analysis of humor in an essay focused on the medieval theory of humors and the mythology of the river-God Achelous.[5] He reminds us that *humor* is cognate with *humid*. In some way humor moisturizes the soul. He notes that in mythology the origins of life are always close to rivers: the rivers of Paradise, the Hindu rivers of Mount Meru, the Orphic rivers of mourning, lamenting, forgetting, and flame. But today the rivers have gone underground, leaving in their place the dry philosophies. "We have lost touch with our sensing of the humors, because our traditional *axis mundi* turns out to be all bark," says Miller with considerable moisture.

Even though black bile produces a dry, cold, remote soul, nevertheless it is still a humor. Ficino compares it to wine. Humor keeps things in motion. Staying close to humor, we are intimate with the directions of the soul and not only in line with the dry patterns of the intellect. Therefore the humor in Sade, black as it is, is important not only to help us have some distance on our own shadows, but also to get closer to the texture of the soul's black needs. It is easy to deny the raven, to opt for green, yellow, and red humors at the expense of the black. Sade performs this service, then, not only to sketch the shadows of civilized, enlightened life, but even more importantly to draw us close to the deep streams that are the source for those significant shadows.

In the face of the dark necessities that life presses upon us, the moralist squeezes his lips together stiffly, while the person who understands life's dark requirements laughs in relief from moralism, in appreciation for the absurd, in the pleasures of power made accessible with the discovery of shadow. When the black river doesn't flow, the shadow-stuff streams out in literalistic behavior: violence, crime, abuse, warfare, the poisoning of the planet.

The image of the four rivers reminds us that black pools at the very origin of things. It is not something to get rid of as though it were unnatural. Psychologically, Sade is a naturalist writer. His steady references to "Nature" truly reflect his appreciation for the archetypal role of black moisture. As repulsive at it seems, life can get moving when the black river is allowed to flow and is even enjoyed. Often, in fact, it is precisely the black that wants to flow, that is stopped up in tight throat muscles that want to shout streams of black emotion, in jittery fingers and hands that want to do black things to good people (hands that have been repressed, not allowed to engage in the work of the shadow), in shifting feet that want to break away from white obligations.

If there is fun in the sickening scenarios that Sade pictures, one after another, and if you can laugh at his absurd fabrications, his fiction is an invitation to break free, at least in imagination, from the chains of pale, moralistic restraint and to consider what pleasures await the liberated human being. When we recall that Sade's fictions are images—powerful, extreme versions of the themes we might find in behavior or more rational talk—his fiction offers a way through the sado-masochistic dilemma. Ultimately, it is the healing of this split that gets the waters going and allows life—yin and yang, light and dark, male and female, doer and done-to—to spill forth.

Woody Allen once explained his occasional ventures into dramatic films as an attempt to portray the tragic side of life. Comedy, he cautioned, can sometimes serve as a shield against those things that we would rather not see. Black humor, which can also be so absurd as to act as defense, has the advantage of being extremely close to shadow. It takes a subtle eye to notice and appreciate it. Sade's humor is full of guile, so that even to laugh at the absurdities he presents, page after page, is to participate in his vileness. This is, then, black bile: a true humor, close to the crap-filled underworld river that somehow sustains life and yet dry in being so far from the more pleasant streams we see in our less Sadeian moments, offering a low, distant viewpoint on the black outlines of everyday life.

Black humor moistens by breaking up the dam made of moralisms and shadows. It takes an appreciation for the Sadeian imagination, for example, to enjoy the films of the Three Stooges. Some people are scandalized and horrified to see adult men banging each other over the head, poking at each other's eyes, applying scissors to their clothes, squeezing a friend's head into a large wooden vise, shooting buckshot at a vulnerable derriere. But this, too, is the shadow side of adult polite society. Do we not do to each other, every day, what these scenes give image to? Many times I have sat in a classroom with my head clamped in the vise of some professor's pet theories, the screws turned tighter and tighter by threat of exam, reference letter, or simple social grace! Don't we do these things to each other all the time: tear away at a public persona, inflict some pain, make a few stabs with pointed words?

The Three Stooges rise again and again, like true clowns, from assault and battery that would do in the average person. They survive, as we all survive the Sadeian pains we give and receive in ordinary life. The clown reveals what is hidden in the everyday world behind a screen of denial. He especially reveals the bruising and frustration that life itself, the ultimate Sadeian libertine, seems to enjoy inflicting upon the human race.

Most problems that people bring into the therapist's office have a Sadeian element in them. A patient, suffering some block or neurosis or symptom, can't laugh at the human condition. Usually he or she can't see that we are all Charlie Chaplin dining on the shoes life offers in lieu of steak. We are also Moe and Curly welting each other with hammers. That is the Sadeian character of the soul, and laughter implies an acceptance of that condition, an awareness that no one is above slapping the face of a brother or twisting the nose of a business associate. From a Sadeian point of view, the Three Stooges carry on the important work of lifting the repression of the ordinary soulful violence of life. They show that we can survive the blows. Recognizing that survival, we laugh with relief, knowing that it is perfectly all right to play the clown.

In his comic poem "The Comedian as the Letter C," Wallace Stevens painted an extraordinarily detailed picture of poet-hero-clown-Columbus-Everyman, including certain descriptions that splash the marquis's imagery on the human soul. He is Everyman, "the Socrates of snails, musician of pears, . . . wig of things." In exotic places,

He savored rankness like a sensualist.
He marked the marshy ground around the dock,
the crawling railroad spur, the rotten fence,
Curriculum for the marvelous sophomore.
It purified. It made him see how much
Of what he saw he never saw at all.

The comic element in Sade is a crucial piece of his vision. Without it his atrocities are mere atrocities, repugnant and alien. But with humor, black and wet, his clownish portrayal of human life offers catharsis. It purifies, making us see how much of what we see we never see at all. Stevens goes on with a variation on the universal refrain he uses to sing of mankind as comedian. He begins with the note "Man is the intelligence of his soil," but later he changes this to "Nota: his soil is man's intelligence." Not only his chthonic nature, but his soiled soul is the source of humankind's intelligence. In this perspective Sade's libertine shares some in the character of Crispin, the Columbus of the commonplace. The libertine strives to fulfill his puny, vile, nauseating desires and in doing so turns his backside to the audience who laugh at him and at themselves.

7.

The Perverted Image

The word *perverted* comes from the Latin *pervertire* which means to turn completely or upside down. Cicero uses the word in the phrase "turning against the will of the Gods." The word can also mean to overthrow or destroy. One of the earliest uses noted in *The Oxford English Dictionary* is from the year 1543 when the word is used of "putting the cart before the horse." We might imagine, then, that a perverted image turns something upside down or backward; it also, etymologically, corrupts and corrodes. It would seem that a perverted image has the power to turn *us* upside down, forcing us to consider experience from an inverted perspective. This may be a disorienting and painful experience, but if nothing else it does offer a fresh point of view.

The Sadeian image is not only an image *of* perversion; the image itself *is* perverted. People offended by perversion want to burn books. It is as though we recognize subliminally that images themselves have penetrating power. In fact, one could make the case that perverted images have special power in a world where images in general are drained of their forcefulness and are manipulated daily for propaganda and advertising. Manipulated images have the narrow thrust of their makers' intentions, a limited capacity compared to images that are pristine. The images of dreams, for example, can move the dreamer into deep emotional states, whether of pleasure or panic. Perverted images, since they are outside the realm of moral acceptance, also retain their primeval power to stir the feelings. Perhaps the strong emotional response to perversion we often see has to do in part with the emotional power of the images themselves.

In an important essay, Niel Micklem writes about "the intolerable image."[1] In addition to offering valuable insights into the dynamics of the potential intolerability of the imagination, his essay also demonstrates the general idea that images have certain classifications and reveal special powers of the imagination. As intolerable images operate in specific ways upon the psyche, so the perverted image plays its own special role. Some of Micklem's comments offer parallel reflections on the perverted image.

For example, Micklem says that intolerable images are not merely irritating. Rather, he says, they might be understood to create "torture that goes beyond the endurance of consciousness."[2] As a source of torture, the intolerable image has a Sadeian element in it. Images that torture consciousness are clearly sadistic, or at least Sadeian, in our technical sense. "The word intolerable," he goes on, "means unendurable to the point where some change is compelled." The intolerable image, therefore, is seen as a goad to change or as an opportunity for psychological movement.

We might consider something similar in the case of the perverted image. The impact on the reader or observer of this kind of image is not as much pain as revulsion. If we could withstand our disgust and let the image penetrate consciousness, our world might be momentarily turned through or inside out or upside down, the cart of our understanding put before the horse. This reversal of consciousness is a technology of vision, an opening to an appearance regularly blocked by a well-ordered, reasonable, and moral point of view. Faced with a perverted image, we feel the strain on our straight and regulated assumptions, but the image demands that the strait-jacket be loosened. If the intolerable image results sometimes in a sudden release of consciousness, the perverted image forces a breakthrough in the moral defenses set up around a particular world-view. Imagination can be constrained by taste, moral narrowness, and control of eros, all of which Sade challenges with his stories of perversion. The pervertedness invites either defensiveness against the image or a stretching of imagination. Therefore it has the potential to heal the soul.

Micklem makes another point that applies, *mutatis mutandis*, to the perverted image. He tells the story of Perseus and Medusa, including the motifs of the sandals of Hermes and his cap of invisibility. In the myth Perseus wears this cap, becomes invisible, and escapes successfully with the head of the gorgon. But Micklem sees Perseus's flight as more than escape. Flight, he says, "is in some way essential to the meeting with Medusa."[3] Flight is not outside the myth; it is part of the archetypal pattern. In a similar way we might imagine revulsion as a feeling and tonality necessary in our meeting with the Sadeian image. Take away revulsion, and the peculiar power of the perverted image disappears. Revulsion is the emotional color of our encounter with this turned-around world. It would be a mistake, therefore, to try to overcome revulsion in order to see the perverted image as actually quite harmless and non-toxic. On the contrary, the stench of a diseased mind behind the Sadeian image helps to preserve it.

The feeling that an image is perverted can stem from moralistic rigidity. To the position that sex is the communication of interpersonal affection, impersonal sex will seem perverted. To the idealization of innocence, Sade's lascivious corruption of the young will also seem perverted. But if we resist the obvious stance in these polarizations, we might see that perversion is a putrefaction of fixed ideas about morality, in the alchemical sense of loosening, preparing for analysis, and deepening. Perversion can be an alchemical ripening of the soul. The process of perversion, Sade's consistent advocacy of evil, serves the polycentricity of the psyche by weakening its rigid, singleminded explanations and values. Perverted images soak the shell of moral defense in the putrid waters of an underworld baptism. At turning points in consciousness, dreams often take the dreamer into foul, wet places where the psyche can mature in rotting fertilizer. A perverted image can be seen as one of the "symbols of transformation."

Morality, defined as an activity of the soul, is the ongoing process of entering into one's destiny and nature with responsibility, that is, with a response in life to the demands uncovered in moral reflection. Gradually during a lifetime, we discover what life demands of us and step by step we deepen our values. Moralism, on the other hand, is some fixed notion about what one's nature requires. Essentially, moralism is a defense against morality, the safeguarding of a single, safe idea about one's life and resistance against the subtlety and complexity of that life. Moralism protects a person from the unfolding of complexity. In moralism there is no evidence of any alchemy ever having taken place. Nothing has been blackened by experience and by stinging reflection. Simplistic interpretations and values of the past have not decomposed. Nothing has ever been dissolved, honestly observed, or allowed to change color and tone in the passing of time and in the crucible of experience.

To this hard, white moralism the perverted image offers a route into complexity. James Hillman's emphasis on psychological polytheism has, among other reasons, the purpose of refining the moral sense, so that depth of reflection rises from the clash of loyalties and understandings. In Sade's perversion the morality of sentimentality meets the anti-morality of cruel nature. Sade's insistence on impersonality, on the corruption of innocence, on sacrilege and impiety, and on the many ways of death splits the sentimental universe like an atom in fission. It disturbs and then deconstructs the habitual moral world, which naturally reacts in righteousness and repression. It might be more precise to call this image "perverting" rather than "perverted." The image itself turns consciousness about, and our indignant reaction to that perversion may be our protective attempt to keep the world in place through all the turns. Something in us, the monotheist and the psychological monogamist, wants to hold it all together under a safe umbrella of unified moral vision. In contrast, one of Sade's many clerical characters, Friar Claude, expresses the Sadeian theology: "Among men the greatest believer is he who serves the most gods." (*Juliette*, 458)

Confession

Perhaps perverted images should always be kept under lock and key. They are ever the foil to the universe that has been accepted and represented without shame or challenge. They thrive in secrecy and inviolability. When they do find their way to the light of day, some of their dark shine breaks loose in embarrassment and guilt, signals that a powerful underworld lurks not far beneath the surface persona. Their expression requires certain genres that respect their vampiric shyness, like confession or pornography.

To confess is to let some of one's own perversion into the light. It is a proper Sadeian genre, complete with masochistic feelings of self-revelation and fear of punishment. The confessional of the Catholic church vividly dramatizes many Sadeian themes: "I confess," "through my most grievous fault." The priest gives a ritual penance or punishment which the penitent must fulfill under pain of hellfire. The ritual is carried out, or was for centuries, in a dimly lighted box, whose architecture would have greatly pleased the marquis and certainly served the soul's need for darkness and enclosure for the preservation of its precious perversions.

There is deep pleasure in confession as well. In *Juliette*, after the young student of horror has been told by Noirceuil that he had dispossessed her parents and then poisoned them, she says: "Monster, you are an abomination. I love you." She goes on: "To hear you confess what you have done sets me all afire, transports me." (149) Confession thrills us as we witness an emergence of deep, perhaps dormant, soul-stuff. James Hillman sees confession as a sacrilegious act, a revelation of fantasies that expose the divine at the innermost level of the soul. We feel shame because we are exposing the divine, the mythic materials that move through our personalities.[4] Confession is not the exposure of ego, although it may feel that way. It is more an opening of a door to the cellar of the Gods. In response the ego is shaken by the red and black glow and the low rumbling voices of that hell below we tend to ignore, knowing at some level that it is always at work stoking the furnaces of personality and behavior.

In another scene Juliette goes for confession to a Carmelite priest in order to seduce him. Toward the beginning of her confession she says, "the pleasure of holding this secret conversation with you is upsetting me, yes, convulsing me, counteracting the effects of absolution." (453) The priest cannot resist her charms, and in no time he is in bed with her. Sade makes one of his more unusual observations, noting that the monk has three testicles. One wonders if he had the trinity in mind, not missing a chance to give theology another touch of shadow.

Another way to restate this passage from Sade is to notice the sexual nature of confession. The small, dark box of the traditional ritual is an objective correlative for the closeness and darkness of any and all true confessing, which is an intimacy with one's own soul. The words "I confess" do not come easily when they are the true conjurers of deeply hidden fantasy or memory. They may be as difficult and as arousing as "I love you." Confession conveys the very seeds of a personality, and so the teller and the hearer are inflamed, like Juliette and the Carmelite, in erotic satisfaction. Sade's erotic images suggest that the unnatural conjugality inspired by confession is not of personalities but of the anima and animus, or some other love figures of the psyche, who approach each other when their profound commonality, usually hidden, is manifested.

Psychotherapists might appreciate both the importance of confession and its Sadeian tone. A person may enter analysis not to examine and repair the problematical elements in life, but simply to confess. Therapy is one of the few structured opportunities for confession, for allowing perverted memories and images to find expression. Sade makes it clear that both the humiliation of the penitent and the power of the one to whom the confession is made are erotic. That is, they serve the soul and therefore fulfill some mysterious desire.

When I lived in a Catholic order where monastic traditions were observed with some strictness, once a month we performed a rite called *culpa*. Several of the brothers and priests would one by one prostrate themselves fully on the floor, rise and kiss the habit of the prior, and then tell the whole community some fault. The confessions were usually not weighty and heart-wrenching, but the Sadeian emotions of humiliation and vulnerability were felt by everyone, not only by the confessors. The superiors—a Sadeian word widely used in religious orders—assumed their exalted roles with unusual ease and delight.

Among the rules of the Sodality Juliette had to endorse was number 18:

> Public confession is made at each of the four major General Assemblies, the dates of which coincide with what Catholics call the four great festival days of the year; at them each Member is in turn obliged to declare in a loud and clear voice by and large everything he has done; if his conduct has been blameless, he is reproved; much praise is his if it has been irregular; be it horrible, if he has accumulated execrable deeds, then he is rewarded; but in this last case he must produce witnesses. The prizes are fixed at ten thousand francs drawn from the treasury. (*Juliette*, 422)

Catholics brought up with the sacrament of confession like to tell stories of searching their souls for good, healthy sins to claim. It seems an insult to confess to the same petty faults every time.

If in Jung the Gods appear in our diseases and in Hillman

they appear in our pathologies, in Sade the Gods appear in our criminal and perverted fantasies. Sade's reference to the Catholic feast days makes clear his intention to supplant Christianity with its shadow religion. This general confession, public, loud, and clear, strongly presents human capacity that is customarily repressed and kept hidden. It is not necessary to see the content of confession as intrinsically evil, but rather as the acknowledgment of loves and necessities of the soul that we do not understand or which simply do not fit in the accepted world-view. This is Sade's fundamental position, stated over and over. If nature has placed some desire or behavior in our hearts, then in some way it makes sense. We may not have the perspective needed to see the value in fantasies we consider perverted, but that does not mean that in themselves they have no worth.

Confession is, as Rafael López-Pedraza might say, the rhetoric, one of the literary genres, of the Sadeian world. Confession is a Sadeian way of speaking, and in a particularly appropriate and effective way it accomplishes Sadeian purposes. The humbling that confession requires is part of its Sadeian texture. The power of the one confessed to is also Sadeian. As I have already pointed out, a clue to the Sadeian nature of an activity is to be found most clearly in symptomatic and exaggerated, literalized forms of that activity. The brutally sadistic inquisitor forcing a confession out of a political prisoner, for instance, betrays the essential Sadeian nature of confession.

Some people confess too much and too often. This symptom suggests a failure to do it effectively. The words must connect with Sadeian feelings of inferiority and humility. When confession is genuine, it may become clear that compulsive confessing was the soul's unsuccessful attempt to express its dark images.

The Pornographic Imagination

If there is a telos in every symptom and if the symptom can be spotted in its literalism, exaggeration, and outrageousness, then the grand success of pornographers in our society points to a powerful need of the psyche for soulful pornography. Our willingness to spend such great sums of money betrays a ravenous hunger for something that actual pornography only approximates. Both the sellers of this genre and those who fight it with passion are caught in this complex, deep quest for a certain style of perverted image. A psychology of pornography requires an approach that avoids both moralism against the image and uncritical acceptance of pornography's conventional forms.

A first move might be to notice pornography's polytheism. In mythology most of the Gods are granted their obscene moments. Aphrodite, of course, most obviously presents the pornography of the divine, or the divinity of pornography. She is shown in sculpture raising her dress, or, naked, looking over her shoulder at her backside, or ineffectively covering her breasts with her hands. Hermes is extremely phallic in his portraits. In the *Odyssey* he appears in the story in which Aphrodite is trapped by her sneaky husband, Hephaistos, while she is in bed with Ares. Hermes tells the Gods he would lie with the Goddess no matter who was present. Even Artemis, the virgin, is shown in stories taking a bath in the woods, surrounded by her nymph companions, but spied upon by Actaeon, the unfortunate youthful voyeur. We have many paintings showing Zeus mating with a swan. Hera, so often righteous and puritan, enjoys a three-hundred year honeymoon with her husband.

Alchemy reconciles the profound dualisms of life in images of the king and queen lying together. In images of the Annunciation, the Virgin Mary is shown being impregnated by a bird, and many of the paintings include the golden stream of semen from the Holy Spirit to the woman, reminiscent of Zeus's impregnation of Danae and the conception of the hero Perseus by a shower of gold. It could be said that the most sacred moments are also the most pornographic, and perhaps the reverse is true.

Where there is strong taboo, certainly there is evidence of some kind of divinity. In Sade the myth that informs all the particulars of his style and the details of his scenarios is Saturnine. The accent is on number, ritual, death, authority—the celebrants are led by bishops, popes, counts, abbots—and an unsentimental tone. Sade's pornography is cold, not like the warm sensuality of Venus one sometimes finds in erotica. It has the brutality that can characterize modern pornography and which inspires some artists and pornographers to create a more humane erotic literature.

But Sade portrays the pornographic side of quantifying, authority, and power. He shows that these, too, can be desired and included in orgy. A person can salivate erotically over numbers, a point that can be demonstrated in any university laboratory. Sade shows that eros can be present in the most unlikely places. Everything has its pornographic potential. Just as Fred Astaire could animate a broom by dancing with it or a wall by dancing on it, pornography can eroticize anything. To limit eros to the things of Venus is to establish a monotheism of the erotic. Traditionally Eros is a daimon rather than a God, a figure between the divine and the human, more an angel who moves between the Gods and Goddesses. While in mythology Eros has a special relationship to Venus and is her son in Apuleius's tale, nevertheless he is available to all the Gods. That is to say, every aspect of life has its inherent eroticism.

Perhaps the most difficult element in Sade—the apparent misogyny, the many tortured women, and the aggressive men—also falls within the scope of eros. The complaint that Sade's pornography is plainly misogynist takes his point of view literally and does not grant his writing the status of fiction. Hatred of the feminine has its place, just as modern feminism gives a place to hatred of the patriarchy. But our own puella nature may require painful initiations of her naivete, too. Our too sensitive soul may have to be toughened by life, put on the rack, her blood let, her limbs tied. Sade's pornography tells a dark and difficult myth that has to do with the necessity of pain and the role of figures in the soul who are fortunately cruel and hard-hearted enough not to be engulfed by sentiment. The tragedy in this misogyny is not its psychological necessity but its literalization in the oppression and abuse of women.

The perverted image is central in Sade's pornography because the essence of the Sadeian work is to turn over the stones of culture to see what life is hidden beneath repression. If we could see through moralism against pornography, we might appreciate the compulsions in it, the craving to see the dark side of the moon, the strong lure of things repressed by the sunny monarchy of ordinary consciousness. It might be better to notice the *context* of the sexual activity in pornography, rather than become focused on the eroticism. The erotic tone shows the attractiveness to the psyche of a certain activity. If we are attracted to images of violence, then we might consider that the soul has a profound need for forcefulness. Pornography provides the occasion for contemplating this object of desire.

Two remarkable events in the life of Sade offer some

background to his particular pornographic approach. The first is the dream he had on a night in February, 1779, of his ancestress Petrarch's Laura. This is how he tells it:

> It was about midnight. I had just fallen asleep with those biographical jottings [his uncle's life of Petrarch] at my side. Suddenly she appeared to me . . . I could see her! The horror of the grave had not changed the brilliance of her charms, and her eyes still had the same fire as when Petrarch sang of them. She was completely draped in black muslin, her lovely fair hair flowing over it. As if to make her still beautiful, love tried to soften the essentially gruesome form in which she appeared to me. "Why do you groan on earth?" she asked me. "Come and join me. No more ills, no more worries, no more trouble in the vast expanse in which I live. Have courage and follow me there." When she said this I flung myself at her feet and addressed her, calling her "my mother," and sobs shook me. She held out her hand to me and I covered it with my tears. Then she too wept. "When I dwelt in that world which you loathe I used to like to look into the future, multiplying my descendants till I reached you, but I did not see you so unhappy." Then I was completely engulfed in my despair and affection, and flung my arms round her neck, to keep her with me, or to follow her and to water her with my tears. But the phantom vanished. All that remained was my grief.[5]

Laura appears to Sade like Persephone, gruesome, dressed in black, enticing him into the realm of death. After this dream, Sade's writing took a new direction away from conventional plays toward his special brand of fiction. As Laura had inspired Petrarch to write of love, this Persephone-Laura led Sade into the infernal world of his strange imagination. Sade writes as one who knows the underworld, as one who might well recognize a mother in this Laura of Death. The pornographic element in Sade's writing could be understood as a vision of the soul from this underworld point of view. Sade's Laura is the shade form of Petrarch's woman. She is Sade's special anima, the darkly beautiful, decaying putrefaction of romantic love. Sade's libertines do not romanticize intimacy and mutual caring because Sade is not Petrarch, and his vision is not about idealization. As he says so many times, his nature demands that he focus his attention on those areas of the heart neglected by conventional attention to the romantic.

Another curious image of Sade's comes from his days in the Bastille at the height of the revolution. Enraged, he grabbed a tin pipe that had a funnel at one end, intended to drain water in the prison, pushed it against the window of his cell, and used it as a megaphone to incite the crowds gathered in those critical hours of revolution. Throughout his life Sade tried to countereducate his countrymen by speaking through the gutters of imagination. If his particular kind of pornography mixes sex and torture, it is not because pornography in general is literally about violence rather than love, but because Sade's anima, the world of mood, desire, and meaning that inspired him consistently, is a Persephone figure, like Kali of the East, whose truth and revelation have to do with the necessity of violence and destruction.

Critics of pornography often deplore its presentation of sex without personality. But that is the point in Sade. Only personalistic morality demands that everything be personal. We can read Sade not as advocating actual impersonal sex, but as showing that something in us desires impersonal connections. Sade's critics in particular complain that his pornography offers a utopian vision of unbridled erotic freedom. But as we have seen, the utopia of Sade, the "no-place" of his rites, is an area sheltered from the limiting assumptions and requirements of accepted ideas and attitudes. When the heart is freed from its benevolent captivity in ordinary morality, then what does it want? Where does its freedom take it? The utopian element in pornography—the impossible sex acts, the unrealistic opportunities—is part of the genre. The pornographic imagination, if only in daydream, creates a world where desire has more effect than it does in an actual world governed by fear of desire.

Critics of pornography also complain about the silly plots and flat characters in books and movies. We see this in Sade. From the point of view of classic narrative form, Sade's stories are unbelievably weak. His characters are allegorical—absurdly artificial and uncomplicated. But again the uncomplicated narrative may be essential to the genre. Even in life, following desire may take us out of the stories we live and away from the continuities and identities that give meaning. In *120 Days of Sodom* especially, Sade abandons plot for ritual tableaux, presenting one scene after another in pornographic shorthand. In Sade's fiction we find anthropological footnotes, perverted theologizing, long lists of rules, measurements of body parts, one-sentence scenarios presenting some absurd sexual arrangement, parodies of philosophy, dialogues more appropriate to the stage than the novel, or simple allegorical names and places. All of these forms seem to inhibit rather than foster movement. But, how much closer to dream are these forms than the tidy narratives of literature. Sade's writing is not poetry; often it is not prose. It seems to belong to the special form appropriate to pornography in which logos is weakened so that eros can be presented without constriction.

Critics also contend that pornography always fails to satisfy.

Readers expose themselves to it excessively because it is never enough. Since pornography is empty, what we need is erotic literature with good stories and characters. But it is possible that the feeling of not possessing the pornographic image and of not being fully satisfied by it is part of this psychological genre. As *pothos*, or longing, is a type of desire in itself, this literature of desire may always feel incomplete. With Sade we are all longing for a vision of the underworld Laura, that mother who would hold our cravings for depth and for the security that only comes from imagination, not life. As confession in Hillman's view reveals the divine mythologies lying in the hidden depths of personality, so the pornographic imagination, in dreams, books and movies, reveals the directions of the soul's desire. This imagery is so far removed from consciousness that it assumes unsophisticated literary forms, seems detached from interpersonal connection, is often tinged with compulsiveness, and seems void of all artistic value. It is not humane, not because it is brute but because it is divine.

Pornography is condemned for focusing on organs rather than persons. Critics say that the mechanical sex of pornography reflects our mechanistic society. But traditional iconography, East and West, has for millennia isolated sex organs and presented the mechanics of sex. People commonly dream of penises detached from the body, or the focus in the dream is on the techniques of the sex rather than the personal feelings. Focus on organs may bring back a sense of organ eroticism, giving body its soul. Much of this kind of rejection of pornography is rooted in perspectives foreign to the genre.[6] Pornography perverts our ordinary expectations, and so we judge it by standards that would preserve the status quo.

It is said that pornography is void of imagination. Pornography is full of imagination, but of a style quite foreign to sentimental assumptions. The pornographic dream, which for many people is the most common genre, stirs the soul. Such a dream clearly shows objects of desire repressed in life, and it also reveals inhibition, guilt, narrowness of soul, and neglect of desire. People whose outward lives seem dry, upright, and almost sexless may have dreams aflame with sexual experimentation. These dreams make it clear that the soul does not worry about the restrictions that channel desire in life. It wants to make all sorts of erotic connections in all sorts of ways.

The word *pornography* stems from the Greek *porne*, a word for prostitute and for selling in general. Pornography makes sex a commodity, and understandably this approach, so contrary to idealized hopes, is soundly attacked. But the Sadeian view is colder. Sex does have commercial value. What would happen to advertisements if sex were no longer treated as a financial commodity? Theology tells marriage partners that they are obligated to give sex to each other. It is part of the contract. Sex, like the soul itself, *is*, from a certain point of view, impersonal. Of course it is something we can offer as a gift as part of our intimacies and love. But, like everything else, it has its valuable shadow side where personalism vanishes.

If we are going to attack pornography, then we have to deal with the spontaneous pornographic productions of the psyche in nightdream and daydream. Like Sade we can say, if pornographic images appear spontaneously, then they must have a place. The very fact that they have such a claim on us, whether we feel their compulsion or are passionate in our distaste for them, demonstrates their power and suggests necessity.

In any case, once again Sade can instruct us to tolerate and find meaning in perverted images. For example, a young man dreams that his body is suddenly extremely flexible. He forms it into a full circle so that he can hold his penis in his mouth. This is a man who had become attracted to a popular cult and had left his family and renounced his worldly life to dedicate himself to the cult's guru founder. The dream might suggest the narcissism and self-sufficiency of the young man's current affections, or it might portray his need to find his own seed from within himself. As is usually the case, the image indicates both pathology and therapy. But it would be a mistake to moralize against this image because of its genre, its pornographic style. Both violence and sex are powerful sources for giving image, not naturalistically but poetically, to the psyche's search for power and pleasure.

The dream is Sadeian in a number of ways. Natural laws are "stretched" for the sake of erotic pleasure, and there is no interpersonal love in this sex. It is an image of uroboric self-containment—the snake sucks its own tail. *Penis* means "tail." Sade explores hundreds of ways of connecting to the phallus. There are few stories in his fictional experiments with sexual congress, but that does not mean there is no imagination. Our stories may keep us within the limits of meaningful sexual possibilities. By neglecting the story element, Sade is free to imagine an infinite variety of connections. In this he is closer to dream than to literature. The young man had no story to tell from the dream about his circle of pleasure, but for him the image served as a stunning icon.

The therapist to whom the young man told the dream had trained himself to respect images, so that even though automatically he wanted to judge the image as the ultimate in narcissistic self-love, he surrendered himself to the perverting power of the image. The dream perverted or deconstructed the therapist's bias against self-absorption. This is how Sade is especially helpful to psychoanalysis, perverting the sentimentality of psychoanalytic theory itself. He approaches an image with a bias toward the perverted, and in that inverted perspective he pulls back the screen of moralism to reveal odd necessities which, when given a moment of acceptance, show their paradoxical but evident validity. The perverted image in pornography is like the miracle in religious history. It forces us out of humanistic naturalism into the mysteries of a world not dispossessed of divinity.

8.

Bonds of Love

A woman who has joined a group of idealistic men and women searching for a vibrant spiritual life has the following dream:

> I am the prisoner of a man. He has many treasures. He ties my hands together at the wrists. I walk down a long hall. He is following me. I try to cut my wrists free on a gold candelabrum before I get to the room where he has a dog waiting to attack me.

With a dream like this, it is easy to identify with the dreamer and feel threat and revulsion. But there is a clue in the text of this dream that hints at something else. The captor is a man with many treasures. Even though he is threatening, he has something of value. Lords of the underworld, like Pluto whose name means wealth, are often described as being both evil and rich. These archons of the underside of life do indeed have treasures, but their gold is a black gold, a corrupt wealth, a range of fantasy and emotion that appears to the topside of life as affliction. Their treasures are vaults of negative feeling and image.

Another clue to the underworld nature of the binding man

in this dream is the dog, an animal often shown as a familiar of Hades. When the dog attacks, the victim is bitten, lacerated, and bled by this animal of the dark. But this attack is not necessarily a negative thing. It could be an initiation into underworld mysteries. Like Actaeon, who was attacked by his own dogs and turned into a stag—the whole event understood by the Greeks as a Dionysian transformative initiation[1]—the dreamer might well be on her way to a loss of topside innocence. Dionysos was one of the Gods of the infernal realm. Becoming attached to the underworld, like joining the Dionysian cult, is a definition of loss of innocence.

The underworld binds us and prevents us from living life as we want to live it. From the underworld come powerful moods and emotions like envy, jealousy, and remorse. These brutal and relentless emotions poison the atmosphere, and they hang around in spite of all variety of techniques for getting rid of them. We are in their bondage and feel an unbearable loss of freedom while in their grip.

This particular dreamer is bound at the wrists. Her bondage prevents her from handling her affairs, from manipulating (*manus*, hand) her environment, from doing the things she wants to do. Her freedom of action is hampered by her bondage. This, of course, is the complaint of anyone bound from within by a mood or desire, and from without by attachment to a person or family. The hands are tied.

In life this woman bound herself to a group of people inspired by a high-minded cause and particularly to a few men who were their leaders. This yoke, therefore, was taken on freely. We all get ourselves into bonds of various kinds: a demanding job, a marriage and family, work projects, financial obligations, or settling in a particular locale. These are all ordinary kinds of bondage. From a certain point of view, life has its Sadeian ways, tying us, limiting us, forcing us to give up freedoms in order to have certain of its treasures. Having a child is a great treasure, but the bondage (we often call it bonding) of child and parent is Sadeian in that it entails painful limitations. Marriage vows are a happy occasion, but they also have stark Sadeian implications.

The dreamer tries to free herself by cutting the cords on a golden candelabrum. One might suppose that insight, even some small measure of enlightenment, might free one from bondage. Here the dreamer finds a valuable golden source of light, but apparently—we don't know for sure—this rich light doesn't work. Psychologically, bondage implies darkness and unconsciousness. The man who compulsively washes his hands several times in an hour is obviously bound to his symptom, but he doesn't know what it is all about. He assumes that if he only had some flash of insight he could get over the compulsion, but he discovers that hundreds of insights do not necessarily bring even a moment of release. The quest for a golden candelabrum may go on for years, but that search could be on the wrong track. We are charmed by light, but the issue at hand—a compulsion, an addiction, or an obsession—is the work of darkness.

If we apply the rule that a symptom is a measure toward healing that doesn't quite work and yet points to what is needed, then bondage suggests the need for being tied and restricted. Maybe the man who washes his hands compulsively is yoked to his symptom because he has not yet submitted to whatever need there is for cleansing. He wants to be free, rather than submit. If bondage is the symptom, then bonding is the necessity. If the man is obliged by compulsion to wash his hands, he may have to give up the freedom of his "hands"—his demand to do whatever he wants—and clean up the fantasies with which he manipulates the world. The symptom suggests that he doesn't feel profoundly clean and so washes and washes in a desperate, empty attempt to find moral purity. Still, his bondage is his avenue toward salvation, if he can only give in fully to the reality to which he is tied.

Religion recognizes the need to be bound to a method. *Yoga* means yoke, a method one takes on and is tied to as part of spiritual practice. In the East, history itself, time in a broad sense, is seen as a yoke, yuga, something to which all are connected by necessity. The only way to make sense out of the psyche's spontaneous fantasies of bondage is to see them in the context of these larger religious images, so that we do not take bondage as a simple neurotic compulsion. Even bondage has an archetypal matrix: it has a telos and points to a necessity. The religions of the world offer insight into profound circumstances in which bondage plays a significant, necessary, and meaningful role. Indeed, the word *re-ligio* means "being bound back." Religion at its core is an ultimate submission and the recognition of humankind's bonding to divinity. Secularism tries to deny that dependence and ends up with human bondage.

To take on one's fate is a necessary bondage. Many times people will complain that they were born into a mixed-up family, at the wrong time in history, in the wrong place. They wish they had been born with gifts and talents they see in other people. Their refusal of fate leads them into envy. Allegiance to one's own fate is a passive position, obviously, and therefore its symptomatic expressions will appear strongly masochistic. The person stricken with envy, a powerfully corrosive and deadening emotion, will often exhibit characteristics of the masochist. But these traits also point to a way through the symptom. In order to be free from the bondage of envy, one may have to submit to the actual limits of one's life and fate and live bonded to one's own nature.

Mythological Bindings

In one of the most frequently portrayed religious scenes of bondage, Jesus is tied or nailed to his cross. Here is an archetypal image of being bound to one's fate. The nails are revered in tradition as holy because they are the means by which Jesus, at times a reluctant messiah, remained loyal, stuck to his mission, and brought his saving philosophy, his gnosis, to the world. His philosophy, furthermore, was an idealistic, puer, rebellious one that not surprisingly brought out the senex binding by his seniors.

Christians meditate on the binding of their savior whenever they contemplate a painting or other representation of the crucifixion. But this sacred binding is especially stark in the traditional "stations of the cross," a remarkable Sadeian ritual contemplating cruelty and suffering in the extreme. In the eleventh station, Jesus is nailed to the cross in unbearable pain. The person who meditates on this station in the passion series feels the full emotion of bondage and submission, reflecting on divinity itself painfully attached to the necessities of human existence.

Sade's narration of the last hours of Jesus is, as one might expect, chilled with black humor. "He is put to torture, he puts up with it. Monsieur his Papa, that sublime God whence he dares affirm he descends, succors him not in the least, and there you have him, this scoundrel, used like the last of the outlaws of whom he was such a fitting chief." (*Philosophy in the Bedroom*, 213)

Jesus fixed to his cross echoes Prometheus bound to his rock. Prometheus is the archetypal humanitarian who steals from the Gods on behalf of humanity. He refuses to be yoked to the divine will and therefore suffers the appropriate punishment: he is chained to a mountain crag, which is the ground of his torture. It is easy to miss the Promethean element in Jesus, perhaps less so in Christianity which sets up a moral system that defies the pagan Gods. But Jesus, too, is a thief, stealing the minds and affections of millions upon millions of people who have dedicated their lives to the particular band of possibility Jesus represents. From the point of view of paganism, Jesus is truly a scoundrel, taking all of religion to himself.

As William Lynch says in his book *Christ and Prometheus*, "one of the prevailing images western man has of himself is of a creature who must live and die unbowed and unsubmissive to the world; it is one of the great stances of Prometheus. This is fine, but it is a polarity, it is not the whole of life."[2] Lynch goes on to search out a way to live in the secular world without being cut off from the sacred, and significantly he recommends that we do this without innocence. Humanitarianism carried out under the illusion of innocence results in profound guilt and in the projection of evil out into the world. "It is only the endless ability of man to defend himself against self-knowledge that prevents the obvious confrontation of secularity with its own evil and that slows its dramatic passage toward its own idea."[3]

Oddly, Christianity's refusal to recognize paganism, a rejection established at the very beginning of its theology, sets it up as a colleague of secularism. It is possible in Christianity to divide life into "This World" and "The Other World." Earthly life can then be lived in a purely secular manner, while religion is given to a world that transcends this one. Thus Christianity becomes essentially Promethean in its impiety in relation to the Gods whose domain embraces the nature and culture of this earthly life. Christianity and atheistic humanism struggle against each other, but they are two sides of a coin as long as Christianity keeps its God in heaven. Sade's comic, acid comments on Christianity are not the remarks of a mere unbeliever; they penetrate to the heart of this religion which might well entertain the images of its shadow that Sade presents so acutely.

A passage in Aeschylus's *Prometheus Bound* carries the humanitarian ideal out to the domain of the divine and down to the deepest pits of hell. Hermes is giving his advice to the suffering, impaled Prometheus:

> At no point can you expect
> an end to that anguish.
> Until perhaps
> A God comes, willing to suffer
> your pain for you,
> willing to sink
> down into lightless Hades and the dead dark
> hollows of Tartaros.

Commentators sometimes take this as a reference to Cheiron, the great centaur healer and teacher who agreed to go to Hades in place of Prometheus. But it may be a statement about all the Gods, a Hermetic intuition concerning the nature of human freedom. Gods also suffer. Jung claimed that the Gods now appear in our diseases, but perhaps as well our diseases are the suffering Gods. Our brash, humanistic efforts toward freedom and self-sufficiency, our Prometheanism, force the archetypal world into a suffering condition, the diseases of our bodies and souls. Cheiron, archetypal healer, is also the archetypal sufferer. The absolute patient is the absolute physician. Or, to put it in another way, our individual and social ills are, from a certain point of view, the Cheironic cure of our devastating, impious Prometheanism.

When we feel the symptomatic bondage that arises from innocent secularism, then we are in a position, like Prometheus chained to his mountain crag, to be visited by the Gods, especially by those Gods, like Hermes, who link the human and the divine, yoking—we might say "religioning" in the sense of binding—our hopes and ideals to the wills of the Gods. Then we might discover the paradox according to which human freedom is most genuine under the conditions of yoga or sacred bondage. Taking on the yoke of divine will, the human being recovers his freedom.

It would seem that Sade fulfills the conditions Lynch requires for a worldly life that is not cut off from religion or its guilt. Sade depicts libertines, those who are working out the freedom to explore their erotic inclination, as bound to those very dictates of eros. They are also, of course, the perpetrators of bondage. Juliette watches as Dame Noirceuil is bound into the service of her libertines: "He placed her in the center of the dining room and immobilized her, her feet were fastened to the floor, there being eyebolts sunk there; ropes attached to the ceiling held her arms raised above her head. As soon as she was thus tied a dozen lighted candles were set between her thighs. . . ." (*Juliette*, 225) The libertine participates in both sides of bondage: he is chained to the whims of his desire, and he binds the feminine element as part of his ritual. There is no split here between sadist and masochist.

Bondage is part of desire. We are bound by eros. The only way we can truly be the objects of erotic designs is to hold still, in one spot, our own free wills stopped. When love blows into a life, usually other activities stop or are hampered. Dame Noirceuil, another of Sade's characters with black (*noir*) in her name (in French her name also suggests "coffin"), is yoked from above and from below. This is the human condition, a caricature or simply a correlative of the celebrated drawing of Vitruvian Man, arms and legs outstretched in the cosmic circle. The dark feminine counterpart of the Renaissance ideal, Dame Noirceuil is tied to the higher and lower firmaments so that her erotic body can be probed and tortured. This anti-Vitruvian woman completes the picture of human life, not only powerful in its humanistic embrace of the cosmos but also submissive as the object of desire, the victim of life's Sadeian inspection. Vitruvian Man looks glorious in his perfect posture, but a Sadeian eye would see that he is also spread-eagled, entirely vulnerable and exposed. It takes a libertine fantasy in ourselves to expose and bind the vulnerable soul for life's play with us. Our soul is the object of life's lust.

Humanism honors the image of the human being gloriously reaching his hands to the edges of the universe. Sade's inverted and completing humanism, not detached from terrifying and mysterious divinity, shows man as clown, eating his feces and fascinated with the rump. Or, he shows us woman suspended in the earthly realm, bound to heaven and hell. His cartoon of the human condition does not thrill the heart and expand the chest. It reveals the other side, that aspect of life we all know in the closed chambers of the heart even as we stand half-revealed in inspiring moments saluting the flag or celebrating a wedding. We know the Sadeian face of human life, but we keep that knowledge to ourselves. Sade had the audacity to go public with secrets usually kept quiet.

The Goddess in Bondage

In Greek religion, statues of the Goddesses were sometimes tied up, apparently in a ritual attempt to curb their powers. Carl Kerényi says that Artemis was known both as "she who arouses" and "she who is bound with lygos vines." He describes a statue of Artemis he observed closely: "The small figure has her arms folded under her robe, behind a cross-binding coming down from the neck in front to the girdle at the back, then to the front again where it is knotted and hangs down—all ingeniously emphasizing the folding of the arms with hands hidden."[4]

Kerényi goes on to depict the bound Hera, Hera Tonea, from *tonos*, cord or rope. These Goddesses were freed ritually by the priestess of the temple, so that both the binding and the liberating were sacred acts. The omphalos, or sacred navel stone, at Delphi and in other places is also decorated with bindings, as though the awesome power of these sacred images required limiting or harnessing.[5]

It is curious that in these ritual examples it is the female deity who is bound and that the binding has reference to erotic power. Artemis raises and lowers the penis. Hera, the divine wife, is both devoted and uncontrollably furious. These widespread religious rituals suggest that even ordinary acts of bondage have a profound archetypal level where they address the needs of the soul. When a couple decides to allow some ritual bondage in their love-making, a rather common practice, then it becomes clear that bondage is more than secular. It is not a literal act of cruelty: the one who enjoys being bound may well press for the rite. It is a dramatic enactment of a longing in the soul. Considering such acts, we tend to focus on the cruelty and miss the specific image—the desire to be bound.

This is not to say that acts of bondage freely entered into by couples do not mirror sado-masochistic issues in life. A man and woman, for example, confess that they feel guilty about it, but they tie each other to the bed sometimes when they make love. As they talk about their relationship, it becomes clear that the power issues are markedly divided and full of conflict. They have prolonged loud and raging fights. Each feels that the other restricts his or her freedom. They give in to each other's demands continuously. They have subtle ways of making the partner feel guilty for demonstrating some authority and power. They moralize each other's actions, and they often retreat in passive-aggressive indirection. The ritual acts of bondage in this relationship are like dreams which depict dynamics at work in life: these rites show in their pleasure that there is a desire to exert and to be affected by power. This is to be expected because the couple does not truly enjoy either side of the power paradigm. The partners exclude Sadeian necessity from life and then ritualize the pattern in the sanctuary of the bedroom.

In Sade it is the woman who is bound. Woman is the carrier of soul, man the visage of spirit. Spirit often aims at styles of consciousness and perspectives that are hampered by the absorbing details of life. Therefore, it seeks out ways to keep the soul in check. We see this especially in those many religious and cult groups organized in the name of spirit that try to bind the soul by having control over the choice of marriage partners, by keeping devotees away from family—giving rise to a whole technology of programming and de-programming, and by subjecting women to various acts of submission, often making them objects of sexual exploration. But these religious groups only demonstrate in an extreme fashion what goes on everywhere—the attempt to keep the soul within limits.

I once attended a meeting of college professors interested in exploring new methods of teaching. Someone suggested that students might relate their dreams in class now and then, and as soon as the suggestion was made, several men jumped up and warned against all the demons that would flood out if this opening to the soul were made. There is a deep fear of anima with her free-ranging fantasies and her apparent threat to ordered reason and behavior. These professors literally leaped into action, offering on-the-spot suggestions for controlling the havoc that would appear with expression of the soul. Without knowing it, they were libertines ready to bind the woman at her mere appearance.

C. G. Jung betrays his fear of the anima in *Memories, Dreams, Reflections* when he discusses her temptations. "What the anima said seemed to me full of a deep cunning," he writes. "Thus the insinuations of the anima, the mouthpiece of the unconscious, can utterly destroy a man."[6] To a consciousness founded in the spirit or animus, the cloud-like fantasies and liquid lures of the anima come as a threat and with great power. In Sade we see the libertine strongly attracted to the female, wanting to inspect her every inch, and yet very much aware of the power emanating from her. He has to tie her down and only then draw close for inspection. Male libertine consciousness pins the butterfly of the soul and then enjoys his utterly powerful inspection of his captive.

This simple pattern is repeated in life again and again when puritanism rules the day, when books are censored, usually because women are portrayed as objects of sexual interest, and when women are excluded from men's clubs. Perhaps there are other fantasies behind exclusive male societies, but one often gets the impression that the female presence in itself contaminates, as though it were a lethal power. It *is* a lethal power, this anima that is carried by women. Its deep moods, its swirling clouds of feeling and fantasy, its invitation to the deep stillness of deathly inactivity and contemplation threaten the particular male spirit of action and understanding.

Ironically, Sade's very words have been subjected to bondage. Once when I was looking for a volume on Sade in a theological library, the librarian checked all the identification cards I could produce and led me to a basement room where I was allowed, in true Sadeian fashion, exactly one hour of study. In some of the books in English, I found several passages were written in Latin. Here he was kept in a basement, shielded from outsiders and hidden behind a language not accessible to most. This is how Sade was treated during his lifetime. The librarian certainly was not aware that his actions were completely Sadeian, that he was fully wrapped in the fantasies he was trying to imprison. All of this suggests that Sade's muse is one of those women who are bound and tortured. His very text is a display of soul that threatens the spirit.

An essay on Sade by Catherine Duncan and Francois Peraldi, "Discourse of the Erotic—The Erotic in the Discourse," focuses on Sade's text and on the "libertinage of reading." The reader participates, these authors say, in the scenarios Sade depicts in relation to the text. "It's not the tight-fitting trousers, nor the body they outline that are erotic, but the deliberate slit made in the material which eroticizes by offering to the view (the reader) what is still half-hidden."[7] Peraldi goes on to describe the reading of Sade, highlighting what we could understand as the anima of the text.

> At the centre of the erotic scene and space assigned to the orgy . . . there are secret rooms, pits, abysses, catacombs, a hole, a yawning gap, where the ultimate rites of the erotic action are performed. From those who descend there, few but the libertine return. In those pits is played out the Unnameable, for this hole metaphorizes a hole in the text. Brought to the edge of the precipice, the text can say nothing more than that there is nothing more to say. And there, where there is nothing more to say, in the bottomless pit where the ultimate act takes place is Death. It's around this empty centre, this pit, this silence of the text that all erotic writing turns. . . . Isn't what we call eroticism this vertiginous desire to be swallowed up, the pull-back and the attraction toward the pit, toward Death, toward the silence of writing?[8]

Listen to this imagery next to James Hillman's description of the anima in which he also quotes Jung: "She makes us unconscious. As she is the very craziness of life, she drives us crazy. 'With the archetype of the anima we enter the realm of the gods. . . . Everything the anima touches becomes numinous—unconditional, dangerous, taboo, magical' (*CW* 9, i, §59)."[9] Sade's imagery takes us to the edge of what is knowable, to the rim of mystery where there is death to understanding and control. Strangely, Sade's fiction is dangerous and therefore hidden and repressed partly because it reveals the power of the feminine. Inspecting those female parts, the libertine is also courting death, the return to the womb, the womb as tomb. The libertine's fascination with the vulva is not simple regression; it is a movement in life that does not follow the fantasy of life by which we must progress, act, and achieve. The libertine is intensely curious about this other path, leading from the external back into the woman's body. Instead of heroically conquering and winning the labyrinthine game of life, he is willing to stop and consider the interior maze of the female. The odd, perverted character of the libertine derives in part from his anti-heroism, his willingness to shut himself away in order to inspect the vulva, an alternative to the phallus as root metaphor of life.

There is, then, every reason to bind Sade, his women, and his fiction. That padlock on the basement room in the library I visited was a prop in the Sadeian drama, of a piece with the ropes binding the hands and feet of Madame Noirceuil. To bind Sade is to recognize his power. The libertine tying up his young woman is acknowledging with his act the power of what she represents and bears. Desire for the woman offers the promise of creation, new worlds, new experience, expansion of self, and so on, but it does so only with the dire threat of extinction. This desire that is so compelling takes its victim to the edge of life and knowledge, turns all moral achievement upside down, and offers a view of life that does not deny death and does not identify only with the victimized soul. There is also aggression, of a non-heroic kind, in his exploration of the woman.

Hillman's analysis of the anima emphasizes this anti-heroic value in bondage. Anima is death to the ego's heroism and in its place offers a different kind of action, one in which ego and anima are *bound* to each other.

> Attachment now becomes a more significant term in anima consciousness than do those more guilt-making, and thus ego-referent, terms like commitment, relatedness, and

> responsibility. In fact, the relativization of the ego means placing in abeyance such metaphors as: choice and light, problem-solving and reality testing, strengthening, developing, controlling, progressing. In their place, as more adequate descriptions of consciousness and its activities, we would use metaphors long familiar to the alchemy of analytical practice: fantasy, image, reflection, insight, and, also, mirroring, holding, cooking, digressing, echoing, gossiping, deepening.[10]

This, says Hillman, is a "consciousness *bound* to life." Madame Noirceuil is bound to heaven and earth, to the Vitruvian round of the cosmos. Libertine consciousness, or the Sadeian imagination, ties its world to anima, life to the woman. The bondage is to the anima and to the erotic passions that swirl around her. The libertine goes deep into the private parts of life and feels fulfilled in the vision he has. Rarely does he want intercourse.

Repression of the Sadeian imagination is a weak attempt to live without bondage, to be free of ties to ordinary life, to find some spiritual way that flies without strings attached. Again and again religious literature of many traditions warns precisely against "attachment," a euphemism for bondage. Hillman's advocacy of anima consciousness is, in a sense, an invitation to bondage. In his essay "Peaks and Vales," he urges a style of consciousness that remains within the valleys of the soul rather than only among the peaks of spiritual achievement.[11] With similar imagery, in another essay, Catherine Duncan advises that "the titillations of pornography stop well below the snowline of these glacial heights of lucidity and white humor."[12]

The person who has dreams and fantasies of bondage, who experiments with bondage in sex, and who gets stuck in painful and disturbing relationships where power is a major problem may need to reflect upon the necessity of being tied to life and fate. Symptomatic bondage suggests a need for submission to eros, to life, to another person. Beneath all the surface and obvious manifestations of masochism, you may see in such a person strong efforts toward control, flight, spiritual avoidance, and occasional outbursts of rage. Such a person appears to need assertiveness and muscle in life. But, in fact, the reverse is probably true. Being attached to the soul, to life, to destiny, to others, to place, to family, or to talent is the kind of submission, limitation, and harnessing that allow desire to perform its rituals of exploration and that invite effective power. Without this bondage, human effort is Promethean, godless, off-track, and soulless.

This bondage of the soul radiates into various versions of itself that appear less symptomatic: attachment, involvement, intimacy, patience, presence, stillness, vulnerability, and self-disclosure. These are all forms of bondage, which, when denied, give rise to fantasies of ropes and handcuffs. As always, Sade is the theologian of hell, speaking for the red angels of the fiery inferno whose job it is to urge and to tempt toward the pleasures of binding and of being bound.

Dreams and rites of bondage, then, are signposts toward a necessity of the soul. Spirit enjoys freedom, transcendence, flight, detachment, withdrawal, solitude, and far-off ideals. But the soul is clothed in the textures and structures of the here-and-now. Fulfilled in attachment, it follows its nature when it is trapped in the labyrinth of time and place. In other words, images of bondage lead the imagination to soul-making—the further binding to fate and nature. Rites of bondage show the way toward the ultimate binding which is religion.

9.

Shadow Therapeutics

One of Sade's most outrageous characters is Comte de Gernande, a "solitary man, a philosopher," fifty years old, monstrously fat, six feet tall, ugly, and fitted out with an enormous nose. His particular libertine pleasures are blood-letting and blood-sucking. He has complete dominion over his wife and has her on a strict schedule of eating and blood-letting. Like most of the libertines he is a monster, but in spite of his ghoulishness we might consider his ministering to his wife as a peculiar kind of Sadeian medicine. The image of the count may even give us some clues as to the role of certain Sadeian elements in psychotherapy.

He appears in the story of Justine, after she has left Dom Severino and the monks of St. Mary-of-the-Wood. Justine is hired to tend to the count's wife. At nineteen, she is the complete captive of her husband, who acts toward her, he says, not out of hostility but from passion. The count's "therapy" is of course utterly revolting:

> Her blood is let once every ninety-six hours; she loses two bowls of it each time and nowadays no longer faints, having got accustomed to it. Her prostration lasts twenty-four

> hours; she is bedridden one day out of every four, but during the remaining three she gets on tolerably well. (*Justine*, 635)

The countess is fed well between treatments to keep her just alive and ready for the next blood-letting. As for the count, he is an epicure of grand proportions. At one dinner he eats two soups, roast beef, eight hors d'oeuvres, five heavy entrées, five light entrées, a boar's head, and sixteen plates of fruit and drinks four liqueurs and twelve bottles of wine. While his wife is always about to vanish into air, he becomes more corpulent with every meal.

The count shares certain tastes with the vampire, and so these winged night blood-suckers offer some amplification for his particular erotic inclinations. Angels of hell, vampires draw the red life-blood from the soul, preparing it for a shade existence of the underworld. The Greek underworld was the psyche's natural home, and it was a bloodless place. Vampires are also allergic to the dayworld of the sun and thrive at night. Their thirst for blood serves the underworld psyche, turning the red literalism of life into the paler hues of that land that lies outside life's affairs. As messengers of hell who attack innocent victims, turning them into the living dead, vampires have a strong Sadeian character; so it is not surprising to find a bloodthirsty figure like the Comte de Gernande in Sade's writing.

In Jung's alchemical studies, blood is the prima materia (*CW* 12, §425) and red the color of sulphur and the sun (*CW* 14, §118). Blood gives image to unrefined life. Alchemy transforms the raw materials of life into more subtle forms. Gross elements of everyday activity turn into imaginal figures and events, and thus soul emerges as a realm of fantasy, mood, and deep interiority. The blood literalism of life transmutes alchemically into the stories and themes of imagination. Vampires, therefore, are technicians of the imaginal.

Alchemy involves a *sublimatio*, a making subtle, effected by the dark transformative processes of mortification and putrefaction. That is to say, soul-making cannot take place without decay and a painful dying to life. The count's strongest desire is fulfilled when he sees his wife's blood spurting in heavy streams from her arms. This image, so repulsive to the literal eye, would fit well into Jung's alchemical illustrations where the shedding of blood signals the violence essential to transformation: a king penetrated with a sword and a serpent crucified, pinned onto a wooden cross. A similar image is the pelican drawing blood from its own body to nourish its young, a gory motif popular in medieval and Renaissance painting. The shedding of blood, exploited by painters for centuries for its arresting color and nauseating allure, can be seen imagistically as a primary component in redemptive or transformative processes. Loss of blood and mortification of the body mean gain of soul.

The count, therefore, performs a special kind of therapy, keeping the wife-soul in a liminal place, barely in life and always on the edge of death. Letting of blood in the name of sublimation requires a libertine fantasy that enjoys and appreciates the move out of life toward death. The libertine also understands that death, or mortification, is not only a natural entropy out of life; it can also be the result of violent action. From the point of view of the *prima materia*, alchemy is a violent process. It cannot take place where life is sentimentally valued over death. Religion, for example, often takes sides in this way with death. Monks and spiritual directors bring a tough-mindedness to their work that allows them to advise their proteges to withdraw, with considerable Sadeian violence, from ordinary life and to cut their blood ties to family and friends in order to become wholly dedicated to the interior life. The move in *Justine* from Dom Severino to Comte de Gernande has a certain logic. It is a short step from the libertine monk to the libertine vampire.

The count's corpulence is a sign of the considerable substance Sade gives the libertine figure. The count gets rich, ample nourishment, while the victim has hardly enough food to stay alive. Psychologically, Sade feeds the image of the libertine and withholds from the victim. He does not nourish or embellish the fantasy of the masochist. In the helping professions, on the other hand, the tendency is to foster the fantasy of victimization. We have more feeling and modes of treatment for victims than for those who commit crimes of abuse. Rather than sharing this bias, the Sadeian perspective acknowledges the necessity and the absolute value of cruelty. Sade gives "weight" to the cruel figure who has sufficient hard-heartedness to take the life blood from his wife, in a sense making her into an anima figure. Sade shows the libertine's cruelty, and then he rewards him with Epicurean weight and riches.

Here we have a first clue in dealing with problems of sadomasochism. If the therapist takes the side of the masochist, he participates in the repression of the libertine. Patients in clinics and in private analysis naturally bring their suffering into the consulting room. Rarely does a person come to therapy complaining of having too much power or success. The therapist tries to be understanding and empathic, which may mean that he identifies with the masochist. The other side, the libertine, is then either completely repressed or is imagined to be coming from the world at large. The image of the masochist is evoked strongly in therapy, but rarely is the libertine made present as a psychological figure having his own necessity and value. We honor masochism with extraordinary compassion, support, and technique. But the libertine is left for dreams in which he is usually felt as a threat by the dream-ego and therefore dismissed too easily as a literal negative element in the psyche.

If the therapist can appreciate Sadeian elements in the work, then he will be able to embrace both victim and abuser in the single archetypal pattern. This attitude keeps the fantasy intact, not splitting the archetype into two literal parts. If the therapist takes sides against the libertine, then the imagination of the problem breaks down, and the therapy is left only with literal mechanics that are acted out within the literalistic split. It is the work of the therapist to keep himself secluded from the actual divisions in life of victim and abuser. The therapist has to do what Sade himself did—remain in the prison of fantasy, cut off from life, so that imagination can be released. To a vampiric (psychological) mentality, blood and imagination do not go together. What happens under the sun is irrelevant, even abhorrent, to inhabitants of Hades. But if the therapist can successfully incarcerate his patient behind walls that shut out literal life, then the patient can also follow Sade's lead and recite a personal catalogue of perversions in an ever-renewed *120 Days of Sodom*. The jailer, therefore, must be conjured. Therapy requires the services of a cold-hearted, incarcerating, dungeon-loving libertine. It thrives on the full-bodied, bloodthirsty appetites of a Comte de Gernande.

Jung describes *mortificatio* as the slaying of the sun (*CW* 14, §168) and as the transformation from a "soiled, imperfect material state into a subtle body." (*CW* 12, §417) The mortifying (making dead) function of the libertine, the passionate work of Comte de Gernande, is an alchemical operation on the soul. Empathy in therapy can be informed by an ego-syntonic fantasy of masochism, which only serves to maintain the complex and to interfere with the important mortifying process. Inspired by dark eros, the libertine effects and sustains the *mortificatio*, helping the life narrative and complaint to break down into deep soul fantasy.

This Sadeian element differs entirely from another approach often applied to masochism. When a patient complains repeatedly of being victimized, the therapist might be tempted to encourage him toward literal empowerment. In other words, the literal sadist might be sought in a program of assertiveness training. But this is not at all the same as evoking the imaginal figure of the libertine. The less literal the libertine is, the more connected he will be to the victim figure. The fantasy of assertiveness denies and devalues innocence. When the libertine is literalized as actual power, innocence goes underground. People trained in assertiveness may show a soulless disregard for ordinary sensitivities, so engaged are they in their willful program of power. Beginning in masochism, they flip over into its opposite, genuine sadism, which, however justified and camouflaged, is nevertheless literally cruel and unpsychological. A corollary in this literalism is the repression of masochism, which appears in the complex with even greater severity than when it is part of the persona.

How, then, do we approach sado-masochistic patterns without getting caught in the complex? Or, another way to pose the same question: How do we bring imagination to symptomatic sado-masochism? How do we cure sado-masochism?

We cure it the same way we cure ham or fish. We put it in a secure, sealed place where it can ripen, putrefy, age, acquire color and taste, and mature. The maturing of sadism and masochism is what this therapy is all about. We might imagine these symptoms as unripened Sadeianism and therapy as cautious incubation.

A cardinal principle in archetypal psychotherapy is to preserve and follow the symptom. This approach avoids the problem of falling into compensatory moves, fighting masochism with sadism and vice versa. If we stay with the symptom, we will not be tempted into compensations and other allopathic remedies that cannot break the seal of literalism. Also, if we take Patricia Berry's advice—that the symptom always has a telos—then we may track the masochism far enough to reach its soul or its gift to the psyche.

Consider the following example. A man wants to get a divorce from his wife of fifteen years, but he can't bring himself to hurt her or to provoke the curses of his family, or hers. He is also afraid that, because of indiscretions in his recent past, if he were to get a divorce he might lose custody of his children. Each time he comes to therapy, he breaks into tears. He sees no way out. On top of all this, he thinks his wife has hired a private detective to watch him. He reports two dreams. In one he is crawling on the floor in front of an Amazon Queen who sits on a throne high above him. In the other a child, holding a gun, stands in front of him and shoots him in the forehead.

Now, should the therapist encourage this man to be strong, hire a lawyer, and stand up to his wife? That would be the allopathic approach. Or, could this man's passivity be treated as *prima materia*, to be placed in a vessel and observed closely? In this latter approach we might find the history of his masochistic soul—other stories telling of the passive, abused figures who have played a prominent role in his life. His dream shows him in an extremely submissive posture in relation to an Amazon Queen. Still following through on the masochism, we might ask if he has submitted to the tough feminine demands of life. Does he really honor women and the feminine? Is there acknowledgment in his life of imagination, feeling, moods—anima? Or does this man's literal weakness obscure his strong resistance to anima?

He says, of course, that he is a model of the liberated man. He shows women too much respect. But, in fact, you see in his manner a strong queenly quality, a signal that the woman of the dream is not really being honored at all but shielded by the psychological defense of identification. You do not have to honor woman deeply if you identify with her. The dream shows both the symptomatic humiliation of this man in the face of the feminine and the gesture his soul requires. The symptom is humiliation; the cure is humbling.

The Sadeian libertine in the man's dream is the child with the gun. The child is turned against him and has considerable power. In life the man uses the power of his childishness to get his way and to avoid responsibilities. But, like a powerless child, he protests innocence. Again the dream hints that his childishness works against him, especially against his thinking (forehead). The dream also hints that there is real power to be found in the child. Heraclitus said that time is a child playing a board game, an image of capriciousness Sade would have appreciated. This man may have to submit to the unexpected and sometimes whimsical, apparently irresponsible turns of fate. His actual childishness also gets in the way of his being more dependent on life and its unexpected arrangements. Yet, contrary to the man's assumption, there is power to be drawn from faithful participation in unpredictable life.

The telos of this man's masochistic weakness in the face

of his wife and fate is a heartfelt surrender to the vicissitudes of life. His habit of collapsing into tears at every thought of entering life covers over the great muscle he flexes as he tries to control every fragment of experience and every person around him. The collapse into emotion severed from thought also indicates his undeveloped and difficult relationship with anima. Obviously he has little trust in the capacity of life to change and to form new relationships and new families. Everything for him has to fit a mental scheme; it has to be thought out completely before it can be trusted. So, the child in the dream wisely aims his gun at the man's seat of intelligence. Here is another image of a violent act that serves a need of the soul.

Sade's Comte de Gernande is not the typical libertine "stud." His phallic nature is wanting, and at the same time his seed is enormous. "The most minuscule excrescence of flesh, . . . what one might find in a child of three was all one discovered upon this so very enormous and otherwise so corpulent individual. . . . seven or eight tablespoons would scarcely have contained the discharge, and the thickest gruel would hardly give a notion of its consistency." (*Justine*, 641, 643)

Because he lists so many variations of libertine behavior and taste, Sade is often compared to Krafft-Ebing, the noted classifier of perversions. We modern professionals, on the other hand, tend to think abstractly, reducing all Sadeian patterns to matters of sadism and power. By turning to fiction Sade is able to specify a carefully articulated libertine world, where not every abuser is strongly phallic and potent. The count's impotence is correlated to an unusually great capacity for insemination. The image suggests that actual impotence, sexual and otherwise, might be related to unusual fertility. So much body and such little phallicism is wedded to a soul always half in and half out of life. Again, more inspiring images of yin and yang—the sacred marriage and the androgyne, for example—tell of important unions, while Sade finds exceedingly odd images for the dark side of conjunction, here a marriage of great body and no-body, of impotence and fertility.

The libertine view is simple and direct, as expressed by Comte de Gernande: "Were it not nature's intention that one sex tyrannize the other, would she not have created them equally strong?" (*Justine*, 647) For Sade it is important for one to submit and the other to dominate. To put it more psychologically, both submission and power have an important place in the economy of the psyche. The count's power is not in his phallicism but in his ample seed. As the castration of Ouranos in Greek mythology results in the birth of Aphrodite, the impotence of the count keeps his wife, his anima, in a soulful, near-death, highly sensitive state. She is one of the kindest and most moving figures in Sade's fiction. We can see her as an image of life on the slender border between imagination and so-called "reality." She may be the artist who cannot find much body in ordinary life or the hospitalized "mental patient" whose soul-work lies in that narrow strait between ordinary life and dying to fantasy. The count's wife gives new meaning to the technical term *borderline*.

The image of the count's impotence is also similar to the masturbation inhibition James Hillman analyzes as a move toward anima and interiorization. Even arguments against masturbation, he says, may stem from "the heroic ego's stance against Dionysian weakening."[1] The count is a "wounded healer," one who is afflicted with failure of phallic power and graced with abundance of seed, and with that unnatural reversal he attends to his wife whom he keeps weak and bloodless. Here is an *opus contra naturam*, the count himself a work against nature, whose function makes no sense from a literal point of view but nevertheless suggests a mysterious truth about weakening and fertility. The therapist, too, in the image of the count, does not have to be supremely phallic in order to serve the soul. In this image the therapist needs ample presence (weight) and a rich repository of seed. In Sadeian therapy, the analyst does not hide himself or withhold his own psychological material, his fantasies and emotions, in order to protect his patient from himself. On the contrary, the therapist enjoys the erotic pleasure of the fullness of imagination and feels free to impose that imagination in the therapy.

Compared to our usual notions of health, physical or psychological, this Sadeian figure is perverted. But, if it is at all possible to withdraw a judgmental attitude from perversion, we may inquire into the need of the soul for weakening and for fertility without phallicism. In our approach to sado-masochistic symptoms, it may help a great deal to keep this correlation in mind. Empowerment is not the only desirable psychological move. "Disempowerment workshops" might be just as important for the psyche as "assertiveness seminars."

Weakness has its own rewards. As it becomes less literally a trait of personality and more a quality of soul, its many forms transmute into more subtle virtues such as vulnerability, openness, the capacity to feel and to be affected, flexibility, and compassion. The count is tenderizing the soul, keeping it in a state of extreme vulnerability. Therefore, he offers an image of a therapist who, by perverting the office, overpowers—that is, gives increase of power to—the therapy with inexhaustible fertility.

Initiation into the Sadeian Perspective

If Justine is the prototypical innocent and the victim of libertine delights, then her sister Juliette is her shadow. She is attracted to the dark practices of the cruel men and offers her own candidacy as a member of their exclusive club "The Sodality of the Friends of Crime." At the age of fifteen Juliette confesses: "I had a rigorous apprenticeship to undergo; these often painful first steps were to complete the corruption of my morals." (*Juliette*, 103) Later, after special training and indoctrination, Saint-Fond says to her: "You please me mightily; your imagination is brilliant, your phlegm in crime is exemplary, your ass is splendid, according to my belief, you are ferocious and libertine; thus do I judge that you possess the virtues I admire." (229)

Juliette gives image to the dark anima, to the delinquent girl of the psyche, the far-from-innocent puella who is capable of extreme cruelty. Sade presents her as corrupted innocence, initiated out of her naivete. Sade himself was accused of corrupting the youth, a charge often leveled against teachers, including Socrates who was executed for it. But, of course, education itself is corrupting, spoiling blissful ignorance and undoing thoughtless convictions. Traditionally initiations are accomplished with blood and gore to emphasize the putrefaction of innocence that every instance of learning implies.

A great deal has been written in Jungian and archetypal psychology about the puer, the boyishness of the soul that is inspiring and problematical. We hear less about the puella and the girlish figures who appear often in dreams and who leave their special marks on a personality. Men and women both become charmed by this girl who giggles through life, or falls into mad, adolescent love, or refuses to see the world as less than an idealized place. In fairy tales she is Goldilocks and Red Riding Hood, innocents exposed to the terrors of the forest. In mythology she is Daphne fleeing from the attentions of Apollo, preferring the naturalness of a tree over the sublime knowledge of the distant God. In dreams she walks downstairs, often into a cellar or cave, and senses danger from the shadows. The naive puella frequently finds herself in the neighborhood of the underworld, as though drawn to her own corruption.

Thrilled with the idea of corrupting the innocent girl, Sade accomplishes his purpose through either torture or initiation. Justine is the eternal victim of shadowy intentions. But Juliette, like a person charmed by the objectionable delights of society's underworld, is drawn to the perverse world-view of the libertine. In order to become a full-fledged member, she has to understand and agree to a long list of rules and principles which serve and protect libertine values. We can see these rules as a corrupting of our own one-sided puella sensitivities.

> Rule 1. No distinction is drawn among the individuals who comprise the Sodality.

This rule simply and concisely formulates an attitude we find throughout Sade's stories: the individual does not count. In our age when the individual is prized so highly, Sade's disregard of the person appears especially perverted. It seems so obvious, too, that, in spite of our stated esteem of the individual, contemporary life is plagued by impersonalism. Everywhere we are identified by numbers—social security, driver's license, bank account. Even at a delicatessen counter we have to take a number. Crimes seem particularly sadistic when the victim is anonymous. Warfare is terrible when faceless people are targeted for annihilation and when armies wear "uniforms," the very word suggesting loss of personality.

Rule number one of the Sodality appears to support this highly undesirable quantification of life. But we have to recall the difference between sadistic and Sadeian. Contemporary life *is* sadistic when it reduces a person to faceless numbers. But is there a way, giving Sade a sympathetic hearing, to find some necessity in impersonalism? Is there a shadow side to our championing of the individual?

In *Re-Visioning Psychology* James Hillman has extensively and passionately critiqued personalism as a theme in modern social science and philosophy. His point is that what we call "person"—our accent on the individual—is a form of monotheism and literalism. Hillman does not equate personhood with ego. Personality resides in the figures of the soul, he says, and in the Gods of myth. But we take all that personhood to ourselves. "We have personalized the *soul*," he writes, "pressing it all into the human being."[2] Anima, he goes on, personalizes existence and teaches personifying by giving image to current emotions and by generating a feeling of interiority. A grounded sense of personality, therefore, comes more from the daimonic nature of our images than from ego or from an overarching, monocentric notion of personhood. In fact, our very insistence on the individual may betray the loss of a sufficiently profound idea of what a person is. Our cult of the individual could benefit from a strong Sadeian critique, so that our notion of personality could deconstruct and resurrect in a more adequate, soulful form.

Again Sade is correct: there is value in subjecting our cherished idea of personalism to criticism. Jung makes a similar move when he advocates a view of the psyche as "objective." His alchemical psychology sees the soul as an object to be considered in itself, cleansed of our personalistic biases. Instead of focusing so intensely on will and ego, a true Jungian approach looks to the psyche as a natural phenomenon having its own qualities. Jung is closely in line with Heraclitus who said: "The psyche has its own principle [*logos*] of increase." Jung gives the example of an idea "occurring" to a person. The person here is not the subject, he says; the idea is. With a similar sensitivity, Hillman has called the psychologist a "naturalist of the psyche." We could look at the stuff of the soul and burn off some of the narcissism inherent in self-analysis. If we could allow Sade to turn our idea of personality upside down, we might also know the soul better and be less shocked by its every turn.

Cicero said that to know a person you have to know the animus, that is, the daimonic figure that drives him and accounts for passion. This, too, like Hillman's emphasis on anima in personhood, is a depersonalization of the ego and a refocusing of the root of personality. There is an element of deflation, however, in this decentralization of the ego. "I" am not as important. I have to look not at myself but at my soul for identity. This is a Sadeian move out of the romanticism of personalism into a colder appreciation for the objective psyche. The process might well wound our narcissism, but, of course, it is exactly such wounding that lies at the center of the Sadeian psychological enterprise.

> Rule 4. The Sodality dissolves all marital ties and ignores those of blood.

Many critics of Sade refer to his strong reaction to sentiment, a favorite theme of his age.[3] On almost every page of his writing he selects a particularly sentimental issue to twist in order to reveal its shadow. Rule number four of the Sodality pulls the rug out from under the most sentimentalized of our institutions—marriage and family. If the rule unsettles, then what it touches is probably the reader's own sentimental attachments to these profoundly soulful and difficult aspects of life—two areas where love and anima meet in deep pleasure and torturing emotional and physical violence.

Once again we can recognize the literal fact that families and marriages have extremely dark shadows which are usually ignored when we praise their high values. A politician has to kiss babies and show off the family in order to be elected. A public figure cannot say anything negative about the family in general and expect public acceptance. But the great shadow of this sentimentalizing appears in mental health clinics and hospitals everywhere—abused spouses, tortured children, and neglected elderly parents. It would seem obvious that, if we did not repress the shadow of marriage and family so much, we might not be drawn into such literalizations of it in our behavior.

But Sade's attitude toward the family in his fiction has more subtle dimensions as well. When the family is romanticized, its members tend to literalize it, so that when a person becomes an adult he may still be attached to the persons and values of his actual family instead of discovering family in a broader sense. The "Family of Man," his own biological family, the family of his interior persons—the metaphoric family is an achievement arrived at through the perversion of the romanticized literal family. In *Love's Body* Norman O. Brown traces a path similar to Sade's. We move from womb to womb, from mother to mother, he says, "and it gets us nowhere."[4] Our wandering is the penis in the womb, he says, the sexual nature of literalistic life. He writes: "The sin in the sex act is not that of love but that of parentage."[5] According to Brown it is possible to be born out of this recurring womb, but that final birth cannot happen as long as we are living the child–parent myth.

Sade's rejection of family is not unlike that of Jesus who, when he was told his family was present and waiting for him, said, pointing to his friends: "This is my mother and brother and sister." (Matthew 12 : 50) His is a Sadeian act, tinged with cruelty and aggression, making the move to the poetic family. The words of Jesus sound harsh, but poetry demands a sacrifice of the literal, a giving up of an unreflected attachment on behalf of a more subtle appreciation for what family means. The sting in such moves is precisely the Sadeian puncturing of beloved literalisms.

Sade's family is a strange one, but it is a family nonetheless. His free-thinkers gather in their dungeons to carry out the dictates of eros which obsess them. Theirs is not a blood relationship—far from it. They are cold, self-absorbed, gathered more for the geometries of their sexual experiments than for any feeling between them. But this is the shadow of family and community. Life demands that we gather together for reasons other than family, for reasons that are impersonal, bloodless, and cold. We gather in a national election, hating each other, but in that hatred finding a correction of values that allows community to exist. Political elections are filled with Sadeian themes and with the language of battle and personal enmity. All communities, from businesses to family picnics, are successful as much for the strife that plagues and incites them as for their warm-heartedness.

The Sadeian family exchanges sentimentality for cold-hearted mutuality in pursuit of eros. This may sound totally uninviting, but consider the following example. Unhappily married for ten years with three young children, a woman has fallen in love with another man who satisfies her needs to an extent she has never known before. She can list dozens of problems with her marriage, a marriage that began without love, in an unexpected pregnancy, and in an atmosphere of insecurity. Now, in every way she wants a divorce, but she cannot bring herself to do it because of the sentimental feelings she has for her husband and her children. She tells stories of her daughter dressed in cute white dresses, smiling at her father. She thinks of mannerisms of her husband, a habit of talking to birds in the morning, and she is thrown into a painful quandary about her future. She is divided and remains indecisive for several years.

This woman does not know the dark beauty of the Sadeian family. She cannot coldly look at her daughter as a person and realize the effect upon her of a mother's sentimental suffering. She cannot see and respond to the demands of her own psyche and her destiny, so blinded is she by the sentimental family. Her dreams reveal the underlying Sadeian thread: she kills her husband and abandons her children. Sade does not present a cheery view of family, but he offers something more fortified than surface calm and pleasant habit.

If we are to follow the lead of our symptoms in order to retrieve soul, then our notion of family must include some abandoning and harsh treatment of the child as well as muscle in our dealings with spouses. Sentimentality about the family can get in the way of necessary strength among family members as they become individuals and break through the shell of family literalism. Sade's break-through, or turning-through (perversion), is absolute, an ontological revisioning of family itself. His iconoclasm offers a way out of the endless births that Brown criticizes, opening up possibilities for living the myth of family more deeply. The brutally deconstructed family is ever ready for further metaphoric application.

> Rule 29. The jealousies, the quarrels, the scenes entailed in love, as well as the language of love, endearing expressions, tender ones, and so on, are absolutely prohibited.

Our "innocent" society is fascinated with stories of romantic love, its entanglements and tragedies. Romance novels sell in the millions, and soap operas run on television for years. Yet, at the same time, we are intolerant of the language of love in the business of life. Love has no place in politics or commerce, and it is a scarce commodity in universities and sciences. Even psychology has trouble with love unless it is sentimentalized in human relations work or "etherized upon a table" for dissection in abstract studies. In society's exclusion of love as a central factor in the working out of culture, we can see society's sadism. The Sadeian redemption of this cold loss of eros lies paradoxically in recognizing the necessity of lovelessness.

The Sodality's criticism centers naturally on expressions of tenderness. From the Sadeian point of view, it is obvious that tenderness has a great shadow and can do the soul serious harm. Juliette is given a "countereducation." James Hillman uses this word to describe the Hermetic indirection in psychological learning and analysis. His words have a Sadeian ring: " 'dissonant learning,' in which the sourness of the student eats through the established positive statements, corroding their face value, yielding an acerbic learning that is *against* what is given, a countereducation."[6] "Dissonant," "sourness," "eats through," "corroding," "acerbic," "against"—this is the vocabulary of Sade. It is not tender. It is not loving in the usual sense.

To Sade loving is important, but it means pleasure in negativity and destruction in the subtlest of ways. For a student to learn dissonantly, against the intentions of his teacher, is to bypass typical tender attitudes toward the teacher and to learn in a condition of tension. The love in a family or between two lovers may find soul in its dissonance as well as in its tenderness. Sade well knew that sex expresses not only feelings of intimacy and endearment but also the tensions and struggles—the aggressive emotions—that keep people engaged with each other.

Juliette—that is, the soul itself in its necessary counter-education—has to learn a natural love of evil. One of Juliette's tutors, Noirceuil, whose name suggests black or heinous crime, applauds her sensitivities: " 'I relish your company. And,' he added further narrowing his eyes, 'you cannot hide it: you are in love with evil.' I trembled. 'I am, Monsieur, I am, very much so, It—it dazzles me.' " (*Juliette*, 148)

People sometimes bring their innocent beliefs and values to psychotherapy and then tell stories of episodes in their lives when they were attached to evil. They felt compelled to steal or shoplift or to embezzle from their company. Or, they are prominent citizens who have an active night life in the dangerous polysexual, drug-filled, crime-prone clubs of a city's subculture. Sometimes women who have been virtuous housewives all their lives fall in love with dark, violent men who teach them in a sometimes painful and physically threatening countereducation the laws of the shadow world they have avoided. Women, too, take a man's innocence into their skillful hands and initiate it in an unfamiliar world of forbidden pleasures. Evil can dazzle the most virtuous of either sex, and that shadowy love and pleasure, that dark eros, can initiate the soul and extend its perimeters. The Juliette syndrome is common among both men and women. Though dangerous, it can be one of the most effective, if darker, ways of soul-making.

If we understand psychotherapy to be about living properly, avoiding trouble, having smooth relationships, and staying on an even keel in career and marriage, then we participate in the repression of pathology. Life becomes humanistically intact and successful, but it is only half lived. A Sadeian element in therapy gives place to shadow without whitewashing it. Sade's fiction can be a guidebook for the therapist, helping establish an appreciation for shadow and for underworld. If we approach the psyche's pathologizing only from the perspective of the humanitarian and health-oriented professional, we fail to grasp the meaning, value, and necessity of the shadow. The resistance we feel to Sade might be identical with our own resistance to the shadow itself.

10.

Sadeian Culture

The ways of Sade are not limited to bedroom scenes of bondage or porno theaters or forbidden books. Any aspect of culture, from the great to the small, insofar as it is engaged in issues of power has therefore Sadeian qualities. Furthermore, since life is never perfect, every aspect of culture will know the split of power into torture and suffering, dominance and submission, or sentimentality and cruelty. The Sadeian paradigm is so fundamental that the simplest object could be analyzed for its sado-masochistic properties. A highway is an invention of massive cruelty, slaughtering people by the thousands. Yet the people who are its potential victims wear it down constantly so that every highway shows its wounds and corrosion. A can of soup is routinely pried open with a violent instrument of torture (from its point of view), and yet it can also poison a person without giving any obvious sign of its danger.

Life itself is both caring and hostile. We are born astride a grave, the hopeful swell of life an inevitable move toward death. Nature is lovely and vulnerable, and yet it is also cold-hearted and cruel, oblivious to human reasons for protection. To live this life with full participation in nature is to adopt its cruelty and vulnerability. Often it seems psychological problems center around this issue of participating in the Sadeian nature of reality. We back away from engaging in cruelty, but the harshness does not go away. We deny the victim our gift of power, and then we become the victims of that denied force. We cannot believe we are capable of the vulnerability a life episode asks for; we retreat and then feel literally and utterly wounded.

Power is a difficult issue in politics, economics, education, medicine, business, family, marriage—in all of life. No one escapes the literal wounds of culture. It is not extraordinary to be taken advantage of financially, to be stopped by the police for a momentary lapse of attention, to be sliced open by a surgeon, to be failed by a teacher, to be subjected to intolerable pain by a dentist, to be sold a defective appliance, to be confronted by a therapist. This is everyday Sadeian life. We are victims and we are perpetrators, all the while participating in the libertinage Sade promulgated as one of the inescapable myths of human life.

About the inescapable conditions of life, Sade offers two perverting points. One is that it is in our nature to be both forceful and vulnerable. There is a chamber in the heart designed for both sides of power. The other point is that eros is fulfilled in the exercise of the Sadeian virtues of coldness, violence, cruelty, and corruption. As long as we see these horrors literally acted out in society and allow others to embody the Sadeian character, we are maintaining a dangerous split and polarization. The innocence that sweeps over consciousness when it projects its own share of shadow on actual people blinds consciousness to its own cruelty. That is Sade's objection to Christianity, not as a religion, but as a point of view, a fundamental fantasy about life that holds blamelessness close to itself and allows others to carry its darkness.

If the individual human soul is torn between victimization

and cruelty, the soul of culture also gets tangled in problems of power. To set the most familiar social activities against Sade's imagery reveals some details of cultural Sadeianism and offers insight into some of the problems that make life painful.

Religion

A few months after Sade's death, the young doctor who had been attending to him in his last days, Dr. Ramon, who happened to be a student of phrenology, made a character analysis based on his skull. One can imagine interest in the skull of a man who had entertained such remarkably obscene fantasies, much like the notion that Einstein's brain must have had special qualities to have produced such intelligence. Dr. Ramon surprisingly concluded that the skull was that of a man of religion.

A case could be made that Sade was above all else a theologian. His writings are filled with theological analysis, from his "Dialogue between a Priest and a Dying Man"—in which the dying libertine corrupts the priest hearing his confession—to many passages in the long novels about Christianity, the pope, monastic life, the life of Christ, confession, morality, universal religious practices, and ritual. But "The Divine Marquis," as he has been known, is not only superficially connected to religion. His work consistently touches upon the taboos which signal the approach of the divine in ordinary life. His Gods are pagan, dark, demanding, and thoroughly unsentimental, and yet it is clear that Sade's imagination is directly informed by contact with an anti-divinity, a horrifying sacredness the civilized world rarely honors.

When culture turns flat and animism gives way to rationalism, violence and sex remain as conduits for the divine. The mystery, the inscrutability, and the power of what is divine break through to consciousness primarily in natural disaster, disease, insanity, and insoluble social ills. We have so humanized and rationalized the positive powers of life that only in pathology does the divine peek through. In this sense, as a bold spokesperson for the deconstructive or perverting force of life, Sade is engaged in the business of theology. Maybe that is why religion has been so concerned to keep him quiet—he is one of their own.

The religious nature of Sade's enterprise and the Sadeian nature of religion are intertwined. Theology, for all its light, is engaged in the dark despotic business of telling people what their lives mean, the morals by which they should live, and the punishments they should expect if they wander from the truth. Fear of the Lord and his preachers is a masochistic experience for the average church-goer, and religious leaders have little trouble playing the role of sadist to the humiliating sufferings in their charges. Many adults enter therapy with fears and guilt that were *inculcated*—a Sadeian word that means "tread upon by the heel"—in Sunday school or in a classroom taught by fervent religious people. *Catechism* in Greek means to "speak very loudly," and religious educators find ingenious ways to get their powerful words deep into the child's psyche. It is not uncommon in certain parts of the United States for parents to send their children to religious summer camps where they are pressured into surrendering their souls to God. These camps have all the trappings of Sade's seraglios—an authoritarian master of ceremonies, innocent subjects and liberated fellows, and forced rites of initiation.

Pain, violence, and suffering are highly visible in the world's religions. The Buddha was concerned with solving the riddle of suffering, and the great vision that first motivated him was the painful sight of sickness, poverty, and death—life's fundamental cruelties. The Gods and Goddesses of the Greeks could be both comforting and cruel. Aphrodite puts Psyche through her painful initiation and is completely cold to her torments. Artemis kills Orion for merely touching her shirt and does not hesitate to send the Calydonian boar to ravage her people. The Inquisition of Christianity sadistically struck fear into pious believers who strayed from a strict line of doctrine. Robert Bellarmine, a saint, arranged to have the brilliant Giordano Bruno burned at the stake after some purifying torture.

For centuries the wounds of Christ were central in the theology and iconography of Christianity. Passion plays, the solemn rite of the *Via Crucis*, the Way of the Cross, and hundreds of devotional books embellish and articulate the precise details of Christ's torture. On St. Patrick's Purgatory, an island of penitence on a small lake in Ireland, men and women, many elderly and infirm, meditate on this passion while climbing with bloodied feet over beds of sharp rocks, fasting and going without sleep all the while. In some countries even today people crucify themselves in imitation of Christ. Internally, many Christians crucify their souls with blows of guilt and rigorous expectations of perfection.

The Sadeian dimension of religion shines forth in almost every rite and prayer. The text of Bach's *St. Matthew Passion* offers a plain, straightforward example of religious masochism:

> I, Lord Jesus, have brought to pass what thou dost suffer.
> His sorrow fills me with joy.
> Thus his exalted suffering must be deeply bitter for us,

and yet sweet.
It is I, I must do penance, with hands and feet *bound in hell.*
The scourges and the fetters, and what thou hast endured, my soul has deserved.
Yes! surely the flesh and blood within us will be compelled to the cross;
The better it is for our soul, the more bitter its impact.

As we have seen, masochism finds its fulfillment in religion. The whole-hearted submission one finds in masochistic behavior ultimately implies a demand for submission to emotion and to fate. The less masochism is lived as a symptom, the more it approaches ultimate proportions and turns into the religious virtues of faith and obedience to one's own daimonic nature. The sentiments of Bach's passion, therefore, can reflect either symptomatic sado-masochism in religious practice, or they may indicate a true religious need for submission. Bitterness does have something to do with betterness, but not in a literally masochistic and moralistic sense. The contemplation of suffering is sweet because surrender to the requirements of our own fate does have its fulfillment. We love suffering, as Sade tried to show, because it is part of the natural world and part of our own nature.

Actual sado-masochistic elements in religion—the authoritarianism of its leaders, the sheepishness of its followers, the hellfire and brimstone moralistic sermons, the strict rules of conduct, even sitting still in church for a longer period than the body prefers—point to the deeper surrender that is the very heart of the religious attitude. Symptoms, however, are raw material. Needing refinement, they can be pushed into the poetic nuances of their core. So, if a particular church or religion betrays strong sado-masochistic elements, however disguised and rationalized, we can see both lack of soul and an opportunity to give soul to that religious experience. Submission to actual religious authorities might be "sublimated," in the alchemical sense of being refined and made subtle, into a deeply felt and lived awareness of the authority of one's own life and imagination, as well as the authoritative character of fate as it "authors" a life. The religious leader who takes this religious authority to his or her own person is transforming the natural—to use Sade's key word—Sadeian requirement of authority and obedience into sadism in the religious figure and masochism in the devotee. The religious figure's strength and endorsement of the demands of a religious path could, on the other hand, evoke the necessary Sadeian conditions of religious feeling. On one hand the difference between sadism and Sadeianism is great, but on the other hand the fall into literalism is easy.

Speaking through the fictional persona of the libertine, Sade's criticisms of Christianity are outrageous and obscene. But such is the rhetoric of his genius. In *Philosophy in the Bedroom* he writes a passage on religion in which he calls Jesus that "clumsy histrionic from Judaea" and his religion "puerile." He approves of atheism and recommends the return of the pagan Gods, especially Mars, Venus, the Graces, Liberty, and Hymen. (302)

We do not have to take these passages of fiction as literal attacks on religion. We might rather learn from Sade to glimpse the shadow in our religious viewpoint, whether we are involved in a religious institution or not. All spiritual effort, aiming at the highest values and aspirations, has within it the danger of excessive purity of intention. Sade apparently had a nose for this "whitening" element in religion, and he responded with caricatures of religion and fictional pleas for a shadow mentality, an awareness of the validity of much of what is repressed in the pursuit of spiritual perfection.

Current popular advocates of spirituality might keep a volume of Sade next to books that sentimentalize the Mother Goddess, or try to redeem the pathologies of this life with belief in past lives, or seek to be spiritually germ-free and uncontaminated by modern culture, or search endlessly for methods of transcendence. Archetypal psychology, with its accent on Greek polytheism, might see the Sadeianism in revived paganism. Perhaps it is essentially Sadeian not to accept monotheism of any kind as a fundamental principle of life.

The sting of psychological polytheism lies partly in its acceptance of otherwise rejected ways of being. Mars with his belligerence and force, Saturn's depression and authoritarianism, and Venus's "venereal" pleasures enter the polytheistic life with impunity. Polytheism also invites tension among these various claims on the soul and a complex, multifaceted view of morality and soul-making. The monotheistic desire for a reliable code of life falls before this fundamental psychological orientation, which perverts efforts toward a single norm of health and behavior. This deep Sadeian hue in archetypal psychology and in other polycentric views of the soul is not a literal weakness, but it does ruin any innocence a polytheistically oriented psychologist might wish to bring to practice and theory. It is Sadeian to defend the lasciviousness of Venus and the steely emotions of Mars.

Sade perverts (deconstructs, exposes shadow, reveals dark eros) all religious ideas and ideals, turning them through to their unexposed sides. Therefore, he is not literally anti-religious but rather serves the religious impulse by showing an opening to divinity and to the angelic order that is inhibited by too clean an approach. Anthropological studies of world religions make it clear that religion as such is not universally without shadow. Sexual orgies, drugs, torture, and dominance easily find their way. But religious monotheism, not only belief in one God but adherence to a narrow religious ideal, rejects many of the thrusts of life as evil. It generates its own anti-religion that is full of power and erotic lure, keeping the Satanic alive and interesting. Religious groups which give inordinate amounts of attention, energy, and money to fight evils like drugs, alcohol, and pornography and which make these anti-values prominent in their publications and sermons are in fact giving religious observance to the rejected Gods of paganism. Sacrifice keeps the Gods healthy, and monotheistic attacks on pagan values thereby preserve paganism, just as the diatribes of the Fathers of the Church give us detailed knowledge about the history of Greek polytheism.

Sade saw the irony in the official repression of his writing and of his person. In 1783 in a famous letter to his wife he notes that repression heats up the very thing repressed, and he offers a more effective way of dealing with untameable eros:

> There are countless occasions when an evil has to be suffered to destroy a vice. For instance, you have got it into your head that you have done wonders, I'll bet, reducing me to frightful abstinence in the sin of the flesh. Well, you have made a mistake, you have heated my head, you have made me conjure up phantoms which I shall now have to realize. . . .
>
> Had I Monsieur No. 6 to cure, I would have set about it in a very different way, for instead of shutting him up with

> cannibals, I would have incarcerated him with some whores, I would have provided him with such a great number that the devil take me if in the seven years he had been inside he would not have used up all the oil in his lamp.[1]

Repression maintains the church of the dark God. From the Sadeian point of view it would probably be unwholesome to lift the repressions: Sade belongs in the protective space of the dungeon. But it is also valuable to be stirred, even disturbed, by the prisoner in cell number six, that figure in every individual and society who reminds us of other Gods and rites which make their claims on human life, whether or not, in Jung's words, the God is called.

Education

We turn to the apparently most benign cultural institutions in order to find the Sadeianism that fills daily life. Education's Sadeian delights are apparent. The word itself, *educate*, has in it the Latin *dux*, leader. The educator is the duke, a word which today colloquially connotes toughness and bossiness. In Sade's rites of torture a duc sometimes is master of ceremonies. Education is also filled with Sadeian language and concepts. For example, it is extraordinarily hierarchical. The presiders are "principals" and "masters." One goes through many years of grades—in fact, we identify children by the "grade" they are in—but a grade is a step in a hierarchy. Then we "graduate" students, using this numerical, hierarchical word for one of the grand fulfillments of life.

Educators pass children and fail them. We subject them

to *examinations*, a word that has to do with weighing. We take them away from the family and keep them against their wills, generally, in buildings isolated in style and geography. Usually these places of education are sparse and severe, not entirely out of the scope of Sade's taste. Education also has a long tradition of physical and sexual abuse. Beating, incarceration after school hours, painful repetitious writing, threats of all kinds, ridicule in front of a class, ignorance paraded in public announcements of grades and punishments, strict curbs on walking, talking, eating, loving, thinking, imagining, daydreaming, and going to the bathroom—education teems with Sadeian methods.

This is not to say that we should find a way of teaching that is free of Sadeian elements. Perhaps the Sadeian factor is essential in learning. The point rather is to acknowledge and to explore this Sadeianism so that we do not repress it with innocent motives and then let it have its literal pains. All learning requires discipline. We call students disciples, but *discipline* also refers to beating oneself with a stick. Once again, the external manifestations of discipline serve as signs of an internal act which is not literally masochistic. A master within oneself can compel the student of the psyche to apply itself to learning. Here sadist and masochist are pure psychological fictions, neither literalized in a person. Of course, it is also possible in an internal way to objectify one or the other and in that way fall out of Sadeian necessity into sado-masochism. A person who feels tormented and obligated from within, from an objectified figure who taunts the soul, has not escaped the literalism of masochism. One can, however, find a saturnine pleasure in study, exercises, discipline, order, numbers, abstractions, rules, and even testing. This is Sade's point, that the limitations and demands of learning can be pleasurable.

One of the characters Justine encounters is Rodin, who is both a physician and a teacher. In Rodin the Sadeian pleasures of discipline are not hidden. His daughter describes for Justine some of her father's methods:

> My father finds in his pupils of either sex objects whose dependence submits them to his inclinations, and he exploits them. . . . Rodin enters, leading a fourteen-year old girl, blond and as pretty as love. He cries, "A note passed to a boy upon entering the classroom!" "Sir, I protest to you, I did not—." "Ah but I saw it dear. I saw it. . . ." Rodin, greatly aroused, had seized the little girl's hands, tied them to a ring fitted high upon a pillar standing in the middle of the punishment room. . . . He snatches up a cat-o'-nine-tails that has been soaking in a vat of vinegar to give the thongs tartness and sting. "Well there," says he, approaching his victim, "prepare yourself, you have got to suffer"; he swings a vigorous arm, the lashes are brought whistling down upon every inch of the body exposed to them; twenty-five strokes are applied. (536–37)

Rodin, you might say, is the inner figure at work in academic discipline. He appears literally in the teacher who does not enter the fiction of teaching and learning but simply acts out the externalized rite. In turn students may take on the role of Rodin's pupil, who in all her blond and luring innocence lives the myth as victim. The myth is literalized partly because of our refusal to acknowledge the Sadeian character of education. We present school as a pleasant place full of good intentions. But everyone knows that violence, power, suffering, and pain are essential to the educational enterprise. As Plato says in the *Epinomis*, "One has first to make acquaintance with life in the womb, then to be actually born, and then further to be reared and educated, all processes, as we all confess, involving untold discomforts." (973 c)

Rodin's rage is inflamed by a note passed in class. Teachers do get enraged by such minor transgressions of school rules, and students are driven to such playful naughtiness. When there is no imaginal participation in the discipline, that is, when it is nothing but external command, there can be little pleasure except to follow the rules masochistically or to rebel sadistically. School vandalism is part of the myth of education.

Sade spells out education's unconscious, its shadow and underworld. After Juliette, a student of libertinage, has been instructed in the many tenets of Sadeian philosophy—there is no life after death, enjoy yourself at the expense of anyone, the soul is nothing but matter made somewhat subtle, God hates humankind and intends to deceive us—her teacher, Delbéne, is happy with her student's progress. "For a libertine intelligence, there is no more piercing pleasure than that of making proselytes. A thrill marks the inculcation of each principle, a multitude of various feelings are flattered by the sight of others becoming gangrened by the very corruption that rots us. Ah, how it is to be cherished, that influence obtained over their souls, souls which are finally re-created by our counsels, urgings, and seductions." (52)

There are several Sadeian themes in this passage that might serve an educator's examination of conscience: the pleasure of making converts to your own style of thinking, the thrill of making your points one by one, enjoying the corruption of a student's unacceptable ways of understanding, watching innocence and ignorance rot, watching a new person emerge who is shaped by your own wishes and understanding and is vulnerable to your seductions. These are essential elements in education, but they are its shadow. When education, following Plato, is described as an erotic endeavor, we might include Sade's dark eros and acknowledge these underworld delights of the Luciferian teacher.

Parents and society as a whole could also examine the shadow in their control of education. A wealthy benefactor of an elementary school checks out the library and finds books that are not entirely positive in tone, and consequently he withdraws his financial support. The school is not advocating his own values, and he is forced to play the libertine lord. In response to objectionable art in a funded graduate school, legislators gleefully withdraw state support, showing the muscle they put behind their views of shaping the minds of the young. Education brings to light Sadeian autocracy one might never suspect amid virtuous support of such a laudable enterprise. But where the Justine syndrome thrives, just there one might expect to find the libertine.

What is the solution to the problem of sadism in education? For one thing, we might listen to Sade as he shouts his vile precepts, catechizing from his prison cell, speaking by means of gutter-talk. When the Sadeian necessities in an institution like education are given no consideration, they thrive anyway as problems that surface from beneath the layer of innocent intentions. If educators had to look at their own desires for dominance, control, brainwashing, and the corruption of youth, their work would become complex and subtle. They might be less inclined simply to act out their prejudices. The very persona of teacher would have darker hues. Students might be less easily seduced into lairs of indoctrination. Even on a national level educators would have to take a self-critical view of their assumptions. Not examining its own shadow, education needs the needling of critics like Ivan Illich, John

Holt, and others who point to the emperor's clothes but who get little attention because their criticisms run into a defensive wall. Educators are so filled with honorable fantasies of their work that there is no room for Sade and his indoctrination of Juliette.

Sade alerts us to the fact that education is by nature full of foul intentions and methods. Simply enlarging our fantasy of learning to include this dark truth would bring soul to the enterprise. Educators could no longer hide their own psychological complexity behind unrealistic values and objectives. If teachers and students know that the pleasures of learning are largely Sadeian, then both sides would enter the work with willingness, vulnerability, strength, and passion. Without having Sade's school in mind, we live a pretense of impossible values and find schools tortured by violence and decay. There can be no true respect and love for an institution that has no shadow. Further, if education itself cannot contain the passions of students and teachers, those passions will likely sear the halls of learning at all levels. Even in the lofty process of education, the Sadeian vision offers promise of soul-making.

Psychotherapy

Like religion and education, psychotherapy has many Sadeian elements covered over by its innocent objectives. Having so much of Justine in its self-definition, therapy is especially susceptible to libertine corruption. The writings of Adolf Guggenbühl-Craig are especially important in this regard, for he is relentless in his analysis of the shadow of therapy. He forces the therapist to consider ugly motives in the most innocent aspects of the work. For example, concerning the fee in therapy he says:

> It is remarkable how often psychotherapists find it necessary to emphasize that the fee is itself a therapeutic necessity for promoting the healing process. May this not be, among other things, a shadow statement? The fee, after all, is not "therapy"; it is there to permit the therapist to live in a manner appropriate to a man of his level of education and training. Here, too, we find a counterpart in the patient. He is often willing to pay a very high fee because it gives him the impression that he is buying the analyst, who, as his employee, will save him the trouble of honestly examining himself.[2]

This critique of psychoanalysis sounds quite Sadeian. Guggenbühl-Craig is not moralizing against the fee; he is simply showing the shadow that surrounds this interesting aspect of psychotherapy. In Sade wealth is on the side of the libertines—even the monks of St. Mary-of-the-Wood. "The four monks composing this brotherhood stand at the head of their order; all belong to distinguished families, all four are themselves very rich, independently of the considerable funds allocated by the Benedictines for the maintenance of this bower of bliss." (*Justine*, 587)

Because psychotherapy is expensive, patients often bring resentment about the fee to the hour of analysis, and masochistically they sometimes feel the sting of the cost of what appears to be an altruistic service. In this sense the consulting room can feel like Sade's monastery and the therapist a Dom Severino. If the therapist refuses to carry this Sadeian shadow, then the soul of the analysis is lost. It is not only that the archetype of healer–patient is split into two literal parts, but the complicated reality of the therapist serving self and other breaks down into a sado-masochistic dichotomy which can appear then in all aspects of the analysis. The piece of soul Sade tried to save in his single-minded fiction is necessary for analysis itself to be psychological.

Sadeian tales are also told in therapy around the issue of power. The patient—the word means "the one who suffers"—comes to the therapist for help. Immediately the therapist has the opportunity to assume considerable power in relation to him. Patients complain about this. Why doesn't the therapist talk about his or her life and problems sometimes? Why don't they become friends and skip the professional arrangement? Why don't they meet in some neutral place?

These suggestions for avoiding the power evoked by setting up the therapy and placed primarily in the person of the therapist are like Justine's attempts to get out of the various dungeons she happens into. Therapy itself has power. It is a Sadeian activity par excellence, akin in this to medicine and education. If the therapist, out of a humanistic concern or a sentimental view of analysis, agrees to the avoidance of power, the therapy stands a good chance of losing soul. The therapist does not have to assume the power narcissistically. But by being strong and by enjoying the authority of the occasion, the therapist can serve the Sadeian needs of the analysis. All genuine power involves *submission* to the source of power. It is not itself sado-masochistic.

Rationalizing away the dependence of the patient on the therapist—agreeing to avoid it if at all possible or finding ways to talk about the analysis without dependence—does not exorcise Sade. Going to therapy, like taking a college course or paying a visit to the dentist, is submission to something that is potentially painful. If the therapist without undue narcissism deeply enjoys the power of the profession, then that power is in the analysis and is available to the patient as well, but only if the patient is willing to submit. As repugnant as are the many scenes from Sade's stories, including disembowelments, hangings, and blood-lettings, they are as much part of soul-making as are the alchemists' separating solutions and blackening ovens. Justine has to submit to the bloodthirsty desires of the libertines if, as a figure of the soul, she is to be opened up, affected, and transformed. We bring our Justine souls to analysis precisely to be penetrated and entered. It is when the patient backs away from submission that difficult, literal, unredeemed dependence appears as the primary symptom of analysis.

All of this is true, of course, in the *fiction* of analysis, as in the fiction of Sade's libertine world. Lose the dramatic nature of analysis and the fictive quality of the principal characters, then the process turns into literal power struggles, dominance, and masochistic suffering. The therapist's power is real but not personal. The point of this power is not to deal with the therapist's personal issues but to evoke the powerful figure of analyst. Patients go to therapy for its power. Otherwise, they would choose a different way of dealing with their problems or their desire for healing. On the surface an odd ideal for the therapist, the Sadeian libertine enjoys power. If we have difficulty identifying with that figure, then our innocence may be too important, blocking an appreciation for authority and forcefulness.

Sade also caricatured humanitarianism. "Among no race that has ever dwelled upon earth," he writes in *Justine*, "has there been any disputing the right to dispose of one's children as one sees fit." (552) A selfless attitude, the fantasy that one is committed to altruistic values, can also help a therapist repress the Sadeian factor in the power of analysis. If the therapist gets caught in the humanitarian response to the abandoned child brought by the patient, the analysis could get stuck in this complex. As James Hillman has written in his analysis of the Oedipus myth, the depriving father figure's many benefits to the child include a corrective to idealizations of the father. Something similar could be said of the therapist. If the archetypal child is only comforted by the therapy, then this child will be "spoiled" and the psyche could remain dominated by untransformed innocence and excessive vulnerability.

All aspects of culture—politics, economics, international relations, business, city planning, transportation, communication, and entertainment—could be subjected to a Sadeian analysis. In all these areas sado-masochistic dominance and subjugation play strong roles. The language of politicians easily slips out of a place of confident power into sado-masochistic bullying. Sadistic governmental displays of force betray the loss of both power and innocence. Economic development sadistically tortures the earth and human populations. Citizens who are forced to breathe poisoned air are victims of sadistic economics.

In extreme, exaggerated caricatures, Sade depicts many of these examples of social libertinage, accenting the desire and pleasure to be found in these acts. Again, even at the social and political level, the solution is to bring soul back by not denying the Sadeian shadow. If we could allow the libertines their place in the remote areas of the psyche, practical solutions to actual sado-masochism would follow. The therapy of cultural sado-masochism is the same as that for the individual person. The work involves an alchemical holding of the Sadeian fantasies and eros, allowing them to tincture values that are colorless and bland since they are without shadow. Innocence itself can be redeemed, not lost, in this process, for innocence split off from shadow is not innocence at all but only a posturing. Paradoxically, embracing Sade could ease conscience and guilt, and it could revivify social justice.

During Sade's last days, while he was incarcerated in the asylum of Charenton, he was obese, almost blind, and asthmatic. He had the companionship of Constance Quesnet, a woman he loved and had lived with when he had been free. According to Dr. Ramon, as quoted by Raymond Lely, "Sade became an important figure at Charenton: parties, festivities, balls, shows, all were in his hands. He chose the plays, some of which were of his own composition, he did the casting, he presided over it all and rehearsed the players."[3] The enlightened director of the asylum, de Coulmier, thought it was fortunate the population included a man who could give stage training to the troubled patients. Sade himself thought of this work as a form of therapy for the denizens of Charenton—art therapy in 1809, directed by the Marquis de Sade!

We have a historical image, then, of Sade the psychotherapist. There is no point in arguing Sade's literal state of mind or his motives, but his story, which history has not been able to sort out easily into fact and fiction, gives us a powerful idea, that the darkest and most perverted haunts of eros have a place in the art of soul-making.

Afterword

Since *Dark Eros* was first published, much has been written and spoken about shadow and eros, and yet I still prefer to learn from Sade how to preserve the soul's love of evil from our attempts to gentrify it. I feel more strongly than ever that much that goes by the guise of intellectual analysis is truly a defense against the ambiguous, ever-changing, unpredictable, and unbaptizable delights of the life-giving but ill-mannered heart. Our task is not to rationalize this evil with the whitening language of psychology, or to integrate it into our personalities so that its black becomes gold, but rather eternally to find ways to allow evil to coexist with our preference for good, darkly infect everything we do and think, and especially reveal its own poetic reading of our lives and its own meaningfulness.

The fundamental paradox, forced upon us in daily tragedies, is the bitter reality that we maintain a world of atrocity by refusing to acknowledge the role of dark desires in our own communities and individual lives. We live a divided life: us versus them, good versus evil. The shadow in human life cannot be brought home as long as we concretize it in some objectionable other. Like everything else, evil is assimilable by soul only after it has been subjected to a poetic alchemy, refined into fantasy and feeling instead of personality and emotion, and woven into the fine tapestry of imagined experience.

It's fine to be imaginative in articulating the details of a sensitive life, but the real nub comes with the presence of aggression, victimization, and power. Will we ever cease reacting to victimization with increased violence? Will we ever realize that strength of heart is to be found only at the deep end of the well of vulnerability? Only the person or nation open to influence, dependent, relying, often disabled can know the deep muscle that grants effectiveness, creativity, confidence, and security. Only the allowance of failure breeds moments of success.

If evil is imagined as other than who or what we are, then it will remain an aspect or segment of life and experience denied to us by the limitations of our imagination. Somehow all that is dark and objectionable has to be seen as material for a full experience of quintessential human life, as well as for the unfolding of our own individual natures. Sade frequently cites the principle that whatever nature has ordained to be possible for human life is legitimate and valid. Taken literally and superficially, this is an absurd law that could be used to justify the most atrocious behavior, but taken more poetically the rule affirms that all that is mysterious can be brought effectively into lived experience. Nothing is unredeemable.

With remarkable consistency, Sade's fiction presents powerful *fantasies* of desire and *images* of sex. It is the nature of fantasy images to depict situations in a way that emphasizes their emotion and disregards their reality component. Dreams, for instance, may place people of different generations in the same setting, thereby increasing the impact of the image while decreasing the life logic. Similarly, in his highly imagistic fiction Sade reveals dimensions of desire and sexuality hidden to a more literal-oriented perspective.

By treating sex as a biological instinct and strong, persistent desire as addiction, we lose touch with the soul of sex and desire—with their depths, their poetic resonance, and the meaningfulness they carry. Sade bypasses natural law and teaches us how far-reaching, how sometimes bizarre, and how important to the heart are desire and sexual attraction. Our usual imageless language for sex and desire serves to protect us from their potency. One protective strategy, for instance, is the rule: Don't act out these desires, they're only fantasies. But we could take a more positive attitude toward dark, erotic imagination by suggesting instead: Take these images deep into reflection, see yourself in them, and find ways to invite them subtly into life.

Sade's fertile realm of eros cannot be inserted into our world easily and neatly. If we see any value at all in him, then we have to make some serious adjustments, not to get rid of evil, but to let it in. Evil is not something to be interpreted to the point where it can be embraced without much commotion. We have to take it on its own terms, and we have to make room for it, which means blasting out some space in our current ways of thought and life for it.

Sex is part of this picture, since most of what sex has to offer is branded objectionable. If we were to live more sexually, we would live very differently. Our culture would take a new direction if it were more erotically motivated. Bring sex back in, and a good measure of soul that has been repressed would come back with it, but the persona we defend so vigorously and so skillfully would disappear.

Sex requires a wide berth in our morality, the image we

have of ourselves, the expectations we have of others, and the way we imagine a peaceable society. Morality is usually perceived as inimical to sex, and vice versa. But what if our morality embraced the vagaries of the sexual passions, and what if morality itself were based on an erotic view of life, and not set up as an enemy to eros? Such an eros-based morality would favor desire, attraction, passion, love, and pleasure, even as it struggled in imagination toward social ways of embodying and structuring those erotic values.

All material of the soul, including the erotic elements, usually appears first as primitive material, raw stuff, the alchemical *prima materia*. Our cultural task is to find ways of housing that raw stuff, giving it a home, and providing it a place within our existent home. This work is analogous to building an altar for a god or creating a shrine for a spirit. This secret, recognized so strongly in fifteenth-century Europe, is that without a concrete home in a cultural setting, such spirits run amok and generate all kinds of trouble.

Alcohol, for instance, is not inherently destructive, but is annihilating if we can't give it form, a context that houses its power. Ficino, among other Renaissance magi, followed the influential passage in the Hermetic *Asklepius* that taught it is possible to make things that house the gods. This is the basis for a Ficinian view of culture, extending to all cultural creations—everything we make and build is a temple for some god or spirit.

Sex requires its altars, its cultural creations, a habitat among human beings. In his extraordinary book *Dionysos at Large*, Marcel Detienne hints at this process in relation to alcohol. Dionysos brings "a fermented drink, which carries with it a madness to be tempered, a savage power to be tamed. Athenian tradition gives us a refined epiphany of the god of the intoxicating cup, making visible the mediations that ultimately resulted in the etiquette of the symposium."* Sex, too, needs "mediations" in order to find a place in human life. The "etiquette of the symposium" is, from another point of view, the rubrics of ritual. With sex, we need to know how to go about it, how to find the forms that nurture the passion and yet give it place.

For all their darkness, Sade's libertines are experts at ritual. They know how to arrange space and time, how to develop architecture and objects, how to dress and how to speak so that eros is served by their perverse etiquette. We, too, need form for our dark passions—language, occasion, place, ceremony.

Sports often represent an attempt at such ceremony, like football players smashing into each other under strict rules, and the brawls of ice hockey, bemoaned but tolerated. The violence in movies also offers some opportunity to contemplate base passion. But one wonders if we do not need more sublimation, less graphic gore and more ritual action. A game of chess can be a Sadeian pleasure, and a Greek tragedy, entered with deep reflection and emotional involvement, may lead us further into an imaginal experience of life's brutalities than the mere visual simulation one often finds in contemporary art and film. In some ways, the pictures of violence we see in movies, with flowing blood and open wounds, serve as a defense against a deeper emotional experience of atrocity—the literalism of the pictures doesn't allow the emotional and fantasy burden of the images to get through.

*Marcel Detienne, *Dionysos at Large*, trans. Arthur Goldhammer (Cambridge, MA: Harvard University Press, 1989), p. 7.

Picture can defend us against image, emotion against feeling, intellect against insight, a dark way of life or personality against soul's unmanipulable shadow, and, of course, psychology against psyche. Sade the writer of fiction has been made into a theory of sadism, and yet his images, short on graphic gore but incisive in their revelation of life's common evil, offer us an artistic mode of contemplation that is not shielded by theory. He is neither a pornographer nor a social theorist, though some have treated him as both. We, too, need not fall into extremes of pornography or theory as we search out ways to open our minds and hearts to the full range of the soul's possibilities.

We can learn from Sade not only the many ways in which dark erotic desires play a role in ordinary daily life, but also the necessity for imaginal representation of those desires. We see ourselves, our souls, in the images given form by the arts, and seeing our souls we can contemplate their requirements. Clearly, we need a full and honest representation of the soul if we are to enjoy adequate contemplation. That is the point of Sade's essay on the novel—that fiction allows us to look at the heart fully.

What stands in the way of this important examination of dark eros? Moralism of all kinds is a major block. Religious moralism is an exploitation of the deep impulse to find an etiquette for our passions. "Etiquette" is obviously too light a word, and yet it suggests the need for limitation through forms that favor social living. Form-giving limitation is not repression, but just the opposite—a means for giving life to passions, ways in which those passions can find expression day by day.

For millennia, religions have offered us powerful images for dark passions, from the sexual extravagance of Indian temples, to sculptural and literary portraits of scandalous Greek gods and goddesses, to powerful depictions in painting and music of the torment and humiliation of Jesus. Stories of the Bible show strong passions in constant play in human life, and yet churches have feared the near-pornography of many biblical stories, which could offer remarkably helpful and profound reflection on passion, and obscured those stories with an overlay of moralistic interpretation.

Psychology brings its own brands of moralism to dark eros. Psychology often implies its belief in the paradise of a hygienic relationship, an adjusted personality, or an enlightened parenthood. Psychology might change radically if it learned from Sade the value of reflecting on fallen human nature. We all eat of the apple, and so we need a psychology that assumes an essential corruption in the human soul and that is not salvational. Psychology seems bent on finding the irreducible crime on which we can lay the blame for emotional pain. This psychology is rooted in a fantasy of original sin, but rather than do what traditional religion has done—told the story again and again of our fallenness—it tries to find a clever way out of that predicament. Yet, to cut out the corruption of the heart is to lose the soul altogether.

How do you present the evil of the heart without fostering its literalization? You don't try to make shadow assimilable. You don't intellectualize the shadow away and cleanse it of its dark emotions. You don't present an ideal of balance, integration, identification, or absorption of the shadow. Instead, you might prepare yourself for a lifetime of struggle with the dark passions, knowing that the crucible of evil desires offers concoctions that have soul. We don't know what will be made when evil is allowed to be itself in relationship to ourselves, but we can trust that whatever appears will not arise from the sentimentalization of experience—the result of a denial of darkness. What appears will have a fullness that is denied us when our psychology is devoted only to the positive virtues.

Interestingly, in Sade evil and desire, or sex and atrocity, go hand in hand. Our intentions tend toward the virtuous, while deeper desire inclines toward the dark. This is a fairly clear indication that the soul longs for its dark sibling, and few have had the imagination of Sade to spell out these lower, less acceptable cravings, and to place eros and evil in such intimate collaboration. Desire and evil, or sex and violence, are an affront to a repressive, life-denying attitude that would like to maintain sentimental life and art; yet they offer a way out of a generally flat and soulless way of life.

In repressive society, decency and pornography feed on each other and give each other a reason for being. Neither represents the soul, which enjoys the rare grounded innocence that comes from the paradoxical embrace of virtue and corruption. It takes a broad and vibrant imagination to hold each within one life, one philosophy, and one sensibility. In that broad imagining of good and evil, one influences the other so that neither is sentimentalized and made into a program for life. In the cauldron of the soul, our innocence is saturated with the acid of evil, and evil itself is corrupted by the desire for innocence.

Most of us know that sex offers exuberant sensations of vitality, but we also know that it asks for a continuous stretching of the structures of life and our understanding. We might like to have both the feeling of vibrancy and familiar structures and interpretations, but ultimately these reveal themselves to be in contradiction. Sade's libertines engage in regular rituals of erotic exploration intent upon discovering ever new ways of satisfying the need for pleasure. Perhaps these rituals say something about the soul's work, its liturgy, as an endless exploration of the demands of desire. Opening up to those desires is the only route to the sense of being fully alive that most of us crave.

Sade also demonstrates in his fiction that to affirm desire fully, and thus allow erotic life full play, includes an aggressive element that, at least in its literalization, contradicts all notions of virtue. He asks us in some way to shut out the world, abandon our parents and families, corrupt innocence, invade privacy, tie up, bind, penetrate, wound, hide, tantalize, and withdraw. If we are to dream Sade's dream onward with the purpose of finding necessary ways to embrace evil, then a major piece in our work will involve a poetic appropriation of these vices. We would have to learn how to be aggressive in these many ways without literalization and identification.

The best way, and maybe the only way, to respond to Sade is to react to his art with art. We need more plays, music, paintings, and films aimed at unfolding his seed vision. We need the alchemy of art to dissolve his challenging images in further pools of reflection. In our individual lives we would also have to discover how to make daily life so poetic that even the most aggressive images in *120 Days of Sodom* would have a place.

I still find Sade painful and shameful to read, and yet I think he is exceptional for showing us ways to imagine evil that in the end will not destroy us. Above all, he teaches us how to imagine evil, how to depict it so that its necessity shows through. We seem to have lost this technique, so relevant to the violence that characterizes our world. Yet, until we have heated our violent ways in steamy forms of imagination, we will be left with its unredeemed literalization. We need a Sadeian vision that embraces the mystery of evil and virtue, so oddly close to the images of the world's religions that one is tempted to revive the tradition of referring to Sade as "the divine marquis."

Notes

1.
Novelist, Pervert, Doctor of the Soul

1. My translation.
2. Letter to Sade's wife, November 1783, quoted in Walter Lennig, *Portrait of De Sade*, trans. Sarah Twohig (New York: Herder and Herder, 1971), 79.
3. Rafael López-Pedraza, *Hermes and His Children*, 1st ed. (Spring Publications, 1977), 102.

2.
Love's Inversions

1. Walter M. Spink, *The Axis of Eros* (New York: Penguin Books, 1975).
2. Leo Steinberg, *The Sexuality of Christ in Renaissance Art and in Modern Oblivion* (New York: Pantheon/October, 1983).
3. *Hesiod*, trans. Richmond Lattimore (Ann Arbor: The University of Michigan Press, 1973), 130.
4. Quoted in W. K. C. Guthrie, *Orpheus and Greek Religion* (New York: W. W. Norton and Company, 1966).
5. Gilbert Lely, *The Marquis de Sade: A Biography*, trans. Alec Brown (New York: Grove Press, 1961), 151.
6. James Hillman, *The Myth of Analysis* (New York: Harper Colophon Books, 1978), 73. ". . . wherever eros goes, something psychological

is happening, and that wherever psyche lives, eros will inevitably constellate." (91)

7. Ibid., 95.
8. Lely, *Marquis de Sade*, 253.
9. Ibid., 256.

3.

The Ravishing of Innocence

1. James Hillman, "The Bad Mother: An Archetypal Approach," *Spring 1983:* 165–81.
2. C. G. Jung. *The Collected Works*, Bollingen Series 20, vols. 1–20 (Princeton: Princeton University Press and London: Routledge and Kegan Paul, 1953 ff.), 12, §152. Hereinafter cited as *CW* by volume and paragraph numbers.
3. Hillman, "Bad Mother," 166.
4. Mircea Eliade, *Myths, Dreams and Mysteries*, trans. Philip Mairet (New York: Harper & Row, 1967), 192–93.

4.

Fundaments and Excrements

1. See Jean Seznec, *The Survival of the Pagan Gods*, trans. Barbara F. Sessions, Bollingen Series 38 (Princeton: Princeton University Press, 1972); and Thomas Moore, *The Planets Within* (Lewisburg: Bucknell University Press, 1982).
2. On this point see the excellent study of Saturn by Raymond Klibansky, Erwin Panofsky, and Fritz Saxl, *Saturn and Melancholy* (New York: Basic Books, 1964).
3. Ivan Illich, *Gender* (New York: Pantheon Books, 1982), 118–19.
4. James Hillman, *The Dream and the Underworld* (New York: Harper & Row, 1979), 184–85.

5. C. G. Jung, *CW* 5, §276.
6. F. Gonzalez-Crussi, "The Dangerous Marquis de Sade," *The New York Times Book Review*, 27 March 1988, 28.

5.
Isolation and Confinement

1. Gaston Bachelard, *The Poetics of Space*, trans. Maria Jolas (Boston: Beacon Press, 1964), 18.
2. See Henry G. Liddell and Robert Scott, *A Greek-English Lexicon* (Oxford: Clarendon Press, 1968), "Chthon," 1991.
3. Quoted in Rudolf and Margot Wittkower, *Born Under Saturn: The Character and Conduct of Artists* (New York: W. W. Norton, 1963), 75.
4. Ibid., 65.
5. Roland Barthes, *Sade, Fourier, Loyola*, trans. Richard Miller (New York: Hill and Wang, 1976), 15–16.
6. James Hillman, "Senex Destruction and a Renaissance Solution," *Spring 1975:* 77–109.
7. Ibid., 80.
8. Ibid., 98.

6.
Black Humor

1. Raymond Klibansky, Erwin Panofsky, and Fritz Saxl, *Saturn and Melancholy* (New York: Basic Books, 1964), 259, quoting Ficino, *De Vita Triplici*, I, 5 (*Opera*, 497).
2. C. G. Jung, *CW* 14, §741.
3. James Hillman, "Abandoning the Child," in *Loose Ends* (Spring Publications, 1975), 43.
4. On this theme see three psychological analyses in *Spring 1987:* Paul

K. Kugler, "Childhood Seduction: Physical and Emotional," 40–60; Robert Stein, "On Incest and Child Abuse," 61–65; James Hillman, "A Psychology of Transgression Drawn from an Incest Dream," 66–76.

5. David L. Miller, "Achelous and the Butterfly," *Spring 1973*: 1–23.

7.

The Perverted Image

1. Niel Micklem, "The Intolerable Image," *Spring 1979*: 1–18.
2. Ibid., 1.
3. Ibid., 11.
4. James Hillman, *The Myth of Analysis* (New York: Harper Colophon Books, 1978), 182.
5. Gilbert Lely, *The Marquis de Sade: A Biography*, trans. Alec Brown (New York: Grove Press, 1961), 217–18.
6. These criticisms are expressed by persons from different points of view in "The Place of Pornography," *Harper's Magazine* (November 1984), 31–45.

8.

Bonds of Love

1. See my essay on Actaeon, "Artemis and the Puer," in *Puer Papers*, ed. James Hillman (Spring Publications, 1979), 164–204.
2. William F. Lynch, *Christ and Prometheus: A New Image of the Secular* (Notre Dame: University of Notre Dame Press, 1970), 18.
3. Ibid.
4. C. Kerényi, *Zeus and Hera*, trans. Christopher Holme, Bollingen Series 65.5 (Princeton: Princeton University Press, 1975), 163–64.
5. Nigel Pennick, *The Ancient Science of Geomancy* (London: Thames and Hudson, 1979), 45.

6. C. G. Jung, *Memories, Dreams, Reflections*, rev. ed., ed. Aniela Jaffé, trans. Richard and Clara Winston (New York: Pantheon Books, 1973), 187.
7. Catherine Duncan and Francois Peraldi, "Discourse of the Erotic—The Erotic in the Discourse," *Meanjin Quarterly* #33: 63.
8. Ibid., 69.
9. James Hillman, *Anima* (Dallas: Spring Publications, 1985), 131, 133.
10. Ibid., 97.
11. James Hillman, "Peaks and Vales," in *Puer Papers,* 54–74.
12. Catherine Duncan, "First Steps in Eroticism," *Meanjin Quarterly* #31, 3: 273.

9.

Shadow Therapeutics

1. James Hillman, *Loose Ends: Primary Papers in Archetypal Psychology* (Spring Publications, 1975), 120.
2. James Hillman, *Re-Visioning Psychology* (New York: Harper & Row, 1975), 48.
3. Ronald F. Brissenden, *Virtue in Distress: Studies in the Novel of Sentiment from Richardson to Sade* (London: Macmillan, 1974). Brissenden points out that the adjective *sentimental* came into vogue in the 1740s, exactly at Sade's birth. (17) "In Sade's view, the sentimental image of man denied not only the sexual elements in his nature, but also his inherent violence, aggressiveness, selfishness, and cruelty." (124)
4. Norman O. Brown, *Love's Body* (New York: Vintage Books, 1966), 50.
5. Ibid., 54.
6. Hillman, *Re-Visioning,* 133.

10.
Sadeian Culture

1. Gilbert Lely, *The Marquis de Sade: A Biography*, trans. Alec Brown (New York: Grove Press, 1961), 252–53.
2. Adolf Guggenbühl-Craig, *Power in the Helping Professions* (Spring Publications, 1971), 42.
3. Lely, *Marquis de Sade*, 427.

Pathology—Classical and Otherwise

Hermes: Guide of Souls • Karl Kerényi

Karl Kerényi, the famous mythographer, classicist and friend of Jung, here presents a beautiful, authoritative study of the great God whom the Greeks revered as Guide of Souls. Chapters on Hermes and Night, Hermes and Eros, Hermes and the Goddesses illuminate the complex role of Hermes in classical mythology, while also providing an archetypal background for the guiding of souls in psychotherapy. A vital contribution both to the study of the classics and therapy of the soul.

149 pp. ISBN 0-88214-224-0

The Love Cure • John Ryan Haule

Because John Haule sees psychotherapy as a very erotic enterprise, this disquieting and provocative book is already highly controversial in the field of psychoanalytical thought. In the profoundly intimate business of therapy, patients allow a therapist to enter the most personal and private reaches of their lives. While patients expose the most touchy and embarrassing details of their innermost being, a therapist's sensitivities, too, get exposed. The intimacy of the occasion is, after all, essential. Haule explores all the elements of the relationship, what draws analyst and patient alike so deeply and so trustingly into each other. Rarely have the erotic dimensions of therapy been so frankly and thoughtfully discussed by a Jungian analyst.

190 pp. 0-88214-513-4

Evil, Sexuality, and Disease in Grünewald's Body of Christ • Eugene Monick

Can there be a Christian Gnostic meditation on Grünewald's Isenheim altarpieceùthe most violently graphic crucifixion in all Christian imagery? From this angle, Eugene Monick explores the interweavings of disease and sexuality within religious mystery. He looks at this sickly Christ that exhibits a suffering mixing Good and Evil in the same body, offering relief to a humanity overburdened with exhortations to carry responsibility for archetypal and pandemic disease. Color plates and a preface by David L. Miller.

189 pp. ISBN 0-88214-356-5

Erotic Poems of the Earl of Rochester • read by Ian Magilton

The Earl of Rochester was Charles II's drinking pal and poet—bawdy, raucous, and yet elegant as only the rakes of the Restoration could be. His poems were long suppressed (but smart schoolboys somehow always managed to find them!). English poetry would never be so outrageousùor funnyùagain. The poems are read by the Obie-award winning Ian Magilton.

1 audio tape: 1 hr ISBN 1-879816-11-3

Gaius Valerius Catullus's Complete Poetic Works • Translated by Jacob Rabinowitz

This bold, yet literal translation grasps the elegance, passion and nastiness not only of the ancient Roman poet but also of first-century B.C. Rome. William S. Burroughs says of this work, 'Beautifully translated...trivial, frivolous, profound, obscene. Hear the fossils of lust." On audio tape: Allen Ginsberg reads selections from Catullus.

150 pp. ISBN 0-88214-220-8
1 audio tape: 35 mins. ISBN 1-879816-03-2

Spring Publications, Inc. 299 East Quassett Road, Woodstock, CT 06281
tel: 860 974 3428 fax: 860 974 3195 e-mail: spring@neca.com